PENGUIN BOOKS

THE BUDGET GARDENER

Maureen Gilmer is the author of seven books on gardening, her articles and photographs have appeared in national magazines, including *Better Homes & Gardens* and *Country Living*, and she has written a series of monthly gardening columns for *Northern California Home & Garden Magazine* as contributing editor. She is also the principal and owner of Professional Landscape Design, a firm that specializes in both residential and commercial landscaping. She lives in Dobbins, California.

THE BUDGET GARDENER

GARDENER

TWICE THE GARDEN FOR HALF THE PRICE

MAUREEN GILMER

PENGUIN BOOKS

PENGUIN BOOKS
Published by the Penguin Group
Penguin Books USA Inc., 375 Hudson Street, New York, New York 10014, U.S.A.
Penguin Books Ltd, 27 Wrights Lane, London W8 5TZ, England
Penguin Books Australia Ltd, Ringwood, Victoria, Australia
Penguin Books Canada Ltd, 10 Alcorn Avenue, Toronto, Ontario, Canada M4V 3B2
Penguin Books (N.Z.) Ltd, 182–190 Wairau Road, Auckland 10, New Zealand

Penguin Books Ltd, Registered Offices: Harmondsworth, Middlesex, England

First published in Penguin Books 1996

10 9 8 7 6 5 4 3 2 1

LIBRARY OF CONGRESS CATALOGING-IN-PUBLICATION DATA
Gilmer, Maureen.
    The budget gardener / Maureen Gilmer.
        p.   cm.
    Includes index.
    ISBN 0 14 02.4704 1
    1. Gardening.   I. Title.
SB453.G535   1996
635—dc20   95-32179

Printed in the United States of America
Set in Usherwood Book
Designed by Michael Mendelsohn of MM Design 2000, Inc.

To my father,
Raoul Paul Esnard,
who taught me the value of fiscal prudence
and solid financial planning

Waste not, want not

PREFACE

The roots of the garden lie in the most elemental parts of the earth, namely sunlight, soil, water, and plants. Up until the past decade or two, little in gardening had changed for centuries except the introduction of a few devices such as the lawn mower. But in recent years a barrage of products, equipment, garden decorations, building materials, and ever more unusual plant varieties have come on the market. Though many of these products claim to work wonders on your garden, save labor, and simplify maintenance chores, in the long run all end up costing you money. It has become too easy to fall into the trap of buying a garden rather than creating one.

Think of *The Budget Gardener* as a toolbox full of cash, because each time you apply one of the ideas in these pages, you save money. You'll find some techniques that are age-old, such as growing plants from seeds or making leaf mold, because both cost pennies compared with the price of container-grown plants or bagged compost. There are also tricks for reusing all sorts of things you'd otherwise throw away. Each item you reuse or recycle into the garden is one fewer thing you have to purchase or pay to dump in the landfill. This is not only good for your wallet, it's beneficial to the environment as well.

Everyone should be able to indulge in the art of gardening without spending. The problem is that the gardening industry has done away with many simple techniques that provide us with the means to garden cheaply, and sometimes free. In their place arise new and expensive gimmicks of dubious value. Certainly there are some things worth paying dearly for, such as quality hand tools or a chipper/shredder machine, which provides a highly productive way to create free mulch from pruning waste. These investments pay for themselves in just a short time. The real budget busters are the continuous nickel-and-dime costs that add up to quite a sum.

Few if any books have ever approached gardening from a financial point of view, but with such a growing industry it becomes essential for us to take a closer look at the details that influence how we garden and why. For the unwary, the simple, rewarding act of creating a garden can easily be transformed by a barrage of new products into a confusing and expensive project. Because beneath all the hype, a garden is still made up of those cheap and often free gifts of the earth: sunlight, soil, water, and plants.

HOW TO USE THIS BOOK

 The field of gardening is so vast, even the most experienced people will continue learning about plants and techniques their whole life through. Garden clubs were once a popular way to exchange surplus plants, new information, and discoveries. During hard economic times such as the Great Depression, some of the most valuable tips were devised to save money. With today's tighter budgets and new ecological awareness, it makes sense to resurrect these old ways and set forth some new innovative ideas so that all gardeners, no matter how little they have to spend, can enjoy creative gardening.

This book is about inexpensive gardening alternatives for beginner and intermediate gardeners. Some of the ideas are relatively simple, others a bit more challenging. Those you choose should be in keeping with your ability and experience. Even expert gardeners can benefit from the tips and tricks of the trade provided here, because there's always more than one way to skin a cat, particularly if it's cheap or free.

Throughout the following pages you'll find boxes that will help you zero in on some of the best gardening ideas to date. Those labeled *Tightwad Tips* contain horticultural instructions related to the chapter topic and special needs of plants. They also point out where it's wise to spend a little more, because in the long run it really pays off.

Beer Budget Items are things you can buy at rock-bottom prices as alternatives to more expensive models or brands. They are your key to special offers and deals from a wide variety of sources.

Finally, *Cheap-scapes Choices* point out where you can find free sources of plants, materials, and literature. These are discoveries I've made during my career as the biggest budget gardener of all.

Consider budget gardening a holistic lifestyle that works on two levels. First, buying smart assures us a larger balance in the checking account at the end of the day. But in addition it encourages us to be more efficient consumers of limited resources, which is everyone's responsibility to the environment. For example, energy and water conservation not only saves us money on our utility bills, it also reduces our dependence on dwindling natural resources. Recycling plastics and organic refuse saves us money, and at the same time lessens the burden of our overflowing landfills. Understanding the true value of the goods we buy ensures that we consume only what is needed without unnecessary waste.

Do not ignore the beautiful books of magnificent colorful gardens, because these inspire and motivate us. But each time you see an expensive idea, chances are you'll find a low-cost alternative in these pages. Keep this book at your fingertips for quick reference, and reread it occasionally as a reminder of all that you can accomplish for pennies. Before you fall into the traps set by crafty advertisers, pause and ask yourself whether a product is necessary and will last. If the answer is no, pass it by and save your hard-earned dollars for more satisfying purchases that are guaranteed to create twice the garden for half the price.

CONTENTS

THE BUDGET
GARDENER

CHAPTER 1

SORTING THROUGH THE GARDEN-SUPPLY MAZE

Guidelines for Economical Tools, Materials, and Equipment

A gardener is only as good as her tools. . . .

Recent studies have shown that Americans spend $75 billion a year on gardening supplies and plants. It is also widely believed that people take greater interest in gardening when they reach their forties, and that is exactly where the baby-boomer generation is today. When this bulge in the population establishes a need for products, the marketplace immediately jumps to fill it.

As a result, there is an enormous assortment of tools and equipment you can buy to create or maintain a garden. Some items are essential, others are a luxury, and still more are frivolous and designed to be purchased on impulse. You can waste a lot of money on unnecessary stuff and still fail to get what you need. This chapter deals with most of these products and points out how to make informed decisions and obtain quality, while parting with as little hard cash as possible.

GARDENING TOOLS . . . AND THEN SOME

A. M. Leonard, Inc., is one of America's oldest garden-tool suppliers, and you would be astounded at the variety of products manufactured for the landscape industry featured in its catalog. It offers more than thirty-six different kinds of shovels, twenty-eight rakes, and eighteen hoes. Many people become so overwhelmed in garden-supply stores they end up buying virtually anything just to get this painful selection process over with.

HAND TOOLS

You hear the word "quality" used frequently these days, and whether you like it or not, that means the item costs more money. Beware of false economy: If you buy a cheap tool and it breaks, you'll have to buy a replacement. This second purchase is usually the quality tool you should have chosen in the first place. In the long run you've paid twice for one tool. So when you find yourself lured by the attractive low price, stop and factor in the price of a replacement.

You can't judge a book by its cover, and this is particularly true when it comes to hand tools. Bright paint and shiny metal have very little to do with quality. Sometimes the only guidelines you can use are the place you buy and the relative price of an item. For example, Smith & Hawken, a gardening-supply company in California, prides itself on its line of high-quality hand tools. You can rest assured anything you buy from them will be top-notch, which takes the worry out of purchasing items from their catalog. Retail outlets are different, because they usually carry more than one line of tools, so price may be the only visible difference among products.

One of the best places to pick up used garden tools of all sorts is at garage or estate sales. In fact, first-time homeowners faced with buying an array of basic equipment can run up quite a bill at the hardware store. But it's not uncommon to find an entire garage full of everything from lawn mowers to pruning shears at rock-bottom prices! These are usually sold at estate sales or by people who relocate out of town or to an apartment and must leave bulky items like hand and power tools behind. Neighborhoods close to military bases and colleges tend to have more transient populations. In fact, one of the biggest secrets among military families is the fabulous base-housing garage sales. Getting on a military base can be tricky if you don't know someone there who can arrange a pass, but if you can manage it, not only will you find garden stuff, but there are all sorts of oddities the GIs have brought back from the far corners of the globe.

SHOPPING GUIDELINES

You'll save a ton of money if you follow these guidelines when you visit the garden center or home-improvement store.

1. **Make a list before you go.** Don't become a slave to impulse items or start browsing and buy everything *except* what you went there for in the first place.
2. **Inspect wood handles.** Tools with very strong, solid-wood handles will hold up for a lifetime if well cared for. Inspect for signs of cracking in the wood and loose connections where wood meets any steel parts. Make sure the wood handle can be replaced if it breaks—it may be necessary to replace the handle a number of times over the lifetime of a tool.
3. **Avoid overly thin blades.** A good pair of hand clippers or long-handled loppers or a pole pruner should have very thick, durable blades. These will have to be sharpened repeatedly, and if they are already thin there won't be much left after a few years of sharpening. Thin blades also bend under pressure, possibly causing serious accidents. This caveat also applies to hoe blades, which are frequently sharpened and won't hold up if poorly made.
4. **Beware of weak metal prongs.** Whether on a cultivating claw, a spading fork, or a bow rake, strong prongs won't bend out of shape or break under pressure. Remember, the soft, crumbly soil at TV gardening shows rarely resembles that of a home garden. Clay can become rock-hard, stony soil is brutal, and adventurous tree roots are akin to steel cable.
5. **Watch out for loose connections.** This applies to that point where the ax meets the handle or the trowel blade meets the hand grip. Imagine raising the pickax over your head and suddenly the steel end flies off to strike a person, pet, building, or automobile! If a tool fails, it often does so where different parts come together, as at hinges, so be sure they are well attached.

**Some of the most highly respected tool manufacturers
you can rely on:**

PRUNING EQUIPMENT: Corona, Felco, Sandvik, Knude
SHOVELS: True Temper, Ames, Razor-Back
RAKES: Ames, Disston, Rugg

BASIC HAND TOOLS AND WHAT THEY'RE USED FOR

This list represents the basic arsenal any gardener or homeowner will need. It's too expensive to buy all your hand tools at once. Most gardeners begin with a few basic tools, then add new ones as the need arises and budget allows. These are the must-haves: To dig and cultivate, purchase a pointed shovel, spading fork, garden hoe, trowel, and hand claw. To gather and move, you'll need a leaf rake, iron bow rake, and wheelbarrow. For pruning, begin with a sturdy pair of hand clippers.

Tool	Dig/Plant	Cultivating	Gathering	Pruning
Pointed shovel	X	—	—	—
Flat shovel	—	—	X	—
Narrow spade	X	—	—	—
Hand trowel	X	—	—	—
Hand claw	X	X	—	—
Spading fork	X	X	—	—
Hoe	X	—	X	—
Narrow leaf rake	—	—	X	—
Wide leaf rake	—	—	X	—
Bow rake	X	—	X	—
Wheelbarrow	—	—	X	—
Hand clippers	—	—	—	X
Loppers	—	—	—	X
Pruning saw	—	—	—	X
Bulb planter	X	—	—	—
Garden cart	—	—	X	—

REPAIR IT . . . DON'T REPLACE IT

We have become a disposable society, but when I encounter an old duff who is still using a pair of shears he bought forty years ago, it reminds me of how wasteful our consumer habits can be. When it comes to gardening tools, you can save a hunk of cash by taking care of them and making a few basic repairs now and then. A quality piece of equipment can last decades. Renovation transforms a battered garage-sale find into a finely tuned machine. Rust is the enemy of all steel products, and wood parts weaken if they are allowed to become overdry from prolonged exposure to rain and sun. During the stormy days of winter, make a point of renovating your tools, using this handy checklist:

1. Use a flat bastard file or a grinder to sharpen the edges of hoe blades and shovels.

2. Sand off accumulations of rust before they go deep enough to weaken the steel. Paint the cleaned steel parts with rust-resistant paint such as Rust-oleum.

3. Replace any wood handles that are badly cracked or broken. If the damage is borderline, protect your palms by sanding the surface smooth, and wrap the handle in friction tape to prevent pinching while in use.

4. Oil wood handles or paint them with weatherproof outdoor latex paint in bright Day-Glo colors that won't get lost in the garden.

5. Tighten any loose connections. Use heavy wire, bolts, and wood screws as needed.

6. Oil any moving parts—hinges, wheels, and so on. WD-40 or 3-in-1 Oil is fine for this.

7. Sharpen cutting blades with a whetstone, or send them out to be professionally done. Replace any blades that are bent, because these will not cut cleanly no matter how much you sharpen them.

8. Be sure all your hand tools are stored away in a dry place for the winter and kept well shaded in the summer.

POWER TOOLS

Buying hand tools is fairly simple and rooted in common sense. But when confronting complicated gasoline-engine power equipment, many of us are truly at a loss. How-to repair manuals for these beasts require a fundamental knowledge of mechanics, not to mention the assortment of tools you need to do the job. Yet it seems no matter how much we study the owner's manual, adjusting a carburetor is still a no-win situation. For as we all know, equipment runs perfectly at the mechanic's shop, but as soon as it touches earth on the old homestead it starts spitting and smoking again, or just ups and dies.

This problem is not about to go away. Rather than continue the struggle, consider a push mower if you have a small, fairly level lawn. These are the same mowers that did the job for homeowners decades before power mowers became widely available. The new push mowers are nearly silent, emit no pollutants, and require no gas or small-engine maintenance. They cut the lawn with a clean scissor action driven by gears that make the job easier, in much the same way gears on a bicycle make it easier to pedal uphill.

But for large lawns, or those too steep for a push mower, power equipment is still the only realistic way to cut the grass. There is now an effort to save the ozone from lawn equipment exhaust pollutants. The Environmental Protection Agency is about to step in and regulate the industry, which guarantees that the price of gasoline-powered equipment will rise sharply, and it is likely there will be no way for the do-it-yourselfer to work on small engines. This illustrates what is perhaps the greatest threat to low-cost gardening today: the regulatory agencies are eager to save us, but it's the American consumer who ultimately picks up the bill.

The power lawn mower has always been the single most important tool for homeowners, and today there are dozens of different products, many of them advertised on network TV. You can spend a fortune on this stuff, and unless you know exactly what you're buying, you can end up wasting a lot of money. Fortunately, the folks at *Consumer Reports* have tested a wide variety of yard and garden power tools to inform gardeners of what is a good buy and what isn't. There are ongoing test results published in their monthly magazine, and you might even check out my book *Easy Lawn and Garden Care*, which contains accumulated ratings of all sorts of power equipment along with lots of helpful tips. You'll find back issues of *Consumer Reports* at the public library, or purchase their annual *Buying Guide*, which has up-to-date ratings.

You may have heard the acronym KISS, which means "keep it simple, stupid," and, oh, how critical that is! Remember when you could look under the hood of a Chevy and easily identify all the parts? The neighborhood mechanic could see the problem and probably fix it in short order. Today's Chevy, on the other hand, is so complex you have no choice but to take it to a sophisticated and expensive mechanic to find the problem, and hope getting it fixed won't put you in the poorhouse. Engines with more numerous or elaborate features are expensive in the long run, because they are difficult to repair. A standard mower costs less to buy and repair than the new mulching mower or one that also vacuums leaves.

Americans are not the best maintainers in the world, because we simply buy a new product when the old one breaks or wears out. But budget gardeners can't afford that attitude. A well-maintained engine can last for decades if it is kept clean and properly stored when not in use, and if gasoline is not allowed to turn to sludge in the carburetor or fuel lines. To extend the life of your equipment and ensure that it starts readily each time you use it, puchase a small-engine manual with detailed instructions on *routine maintenance*. Read and follow the directions diligently.

There are certain power tools that may be as indispensable as the lawn mower, depending on what kind of landscape you have. Lawns must be neatly edged if they are to appear tidy, and edging them by hand with manual scissor tools is a difficult, time-consuming job. Edging can also be done with a specialized tool with a blade that adds yet another piece of gasoline-powered equipment to maintain. The use of power edgers has declined since the invention of more versatile string trimmers (such as Weed Eater), which not only cut down unwanted weeds elsewhere but are also used to edge the lawn—although this is not recommended by most manufacturers. Newer models have safe edging features, besides their numerous other capabilities. This dual use, plus the fact that some brands can be powered by electricity, makes them a bargain compared with traditional edgers.

For gardens with extensive hedges or topiary, the laborious task of hand shearing makes a power hedge clipper worth its weight in gold. Though more expensive than a manual one, a power hedge clipper not only saves time but actually does a better job than manual clippers. Most power clippers are electric, but there are some with small gasoline engines; these come in handy for big hedge jobs far from a power source. The electric tools are not very expensive to buy and often show up at garage sales.

For large homesites on forested land or where there are lots of older shade trees on the property, there is a frequent need to prune larger limbs or cut up fallen ones. Though this can be done with a manual pruning saw, chain saws do the job quickly and with little effort. A gasoline-powered chain saw can be difficult to maintain, especially if you aren't mechanically inclined. Fortunately, small electric models are now widely available at a reasonable price, and best of all, some are designed to be attached to a long pole for overhead jobs. For those who lack physical strength, these small power saws come in handy for all sorts of tasks and are a wise investment.

Before you invest in specialized equipment such as a rototiller or chipper/shredder, be sure you will use it enough to make the price worthwhile. For example, if you use a rototiller just once or twice a year in the vegetable garden, the rest of the time it just sits and becomes a devil to start up again. It's simpler and a lot cheaper to rent the tiller for spring and fall cultivation. On the other hand, if you're an avid organic gardener and maintain a veggie plot most of the year, having the tiller at your fingertips allows you to prepare the soil for planting anytime.

Chipper/shredders are invaluable for creating mulches and compost out of waste, particularly in the fall. You must buy a powerful unit to do the tasks shown on television ads, and there are many brands on the market that just aren't strong enough and may break down. Therefore, unless you buy the expensive top-of-the-line unit, chances are it won't last and you'll be out a lot of money. You may be better off renting.

One option is to form a cooperative with your neighbors and share certain pieces of equipment. This is not a new idea, because farmers have historically shared harvesting equipment. The only difficulty is that not everyone will treat the equipment with equal care, and if repairs are needed, particularly with gasoline engines, there could be disputes. Barring any such disagreements, the best tools to share are those used occasionally, such as the rototiller, chipper/shredder, and chain saw.

GARDEN PRODUCTS GALORE

When you enter the garden department of a home-improvement store you may be overwhelmed by the array of boxes and bags of materials. The packaging is just like that of supermarket food products, with bright colors and bold graphics to catch your eye. But if you look closely, you'll find that virtually all of them can be categorized as either a fertilizer, pest-control product, or weed killer. And as in the grocery store, there are name brands and generic alternatives.

Most people closely inspect the ingredients labels on food products, the weight of the contents, and the price. This method should also apply to most garden products. All fertilizers are labeled with three numbers that explain the potency of nitrogen, phosphorus, and potassium—the basic nutrients plants need—in terms of the percentage of each ingredient per pound. Treat these numbers as you would the ingredients list on a food-product label and use them to compare prices.

To translate this idea into garden terms, for $7 you can buy 2 pounds of special rose formula fertilizer (20–15–10), which contains 20 percent nitrogen, 15 percent phosphorus, and 10 percent potassium. There might be a trace of sulfur or iron in there too, whether your soil needs it or not. This works out to about $3.50 per pound of product, and manufacturers know a 2-pound container will fit nicely on the shelf at eye level.

Now look for the larger bags of granular fertilizer sometimes stored outdoors or under display tables away from the smaller, more costly products on the shelves. Look at the formula label on each bag and find one that is close to the same percentages on the special rose food. You might find something similar, such as 23–16–8, priced at $10 for a 20-pound bag. Sure, it isn't labeled with fancy colors, nor does it say rose food on the bag, yet its contents are nearly identical to the special formula for roses. At this price you pay roughly 50 cents per pound!

It doesn't take a brain surgeon to see the giant difference in price for virtually the same product. Any experienced rose aficionado will tell you that these plants are heavy feeders and a 2-pound can won't go very far. If you look in a rose lover's garden shed, you're sure to find the less expensive, generic 20-pound bag, or perhaps a 50-pound bag that offers even more savings.

FRUGAL FERTILIZERS

Because fertilizers speed plant growth and compensate for poor soil, they are by far the most widely used gardening products. Unlike chemical weed- and pest-control products, these must be applied repeatedly throughout the growing season for best results. Strict organic gardeners should skip this section and refer to the soil improvers detailed in Chapter 2.

By and large, most homeowners use chemical fertilizers that are basically plant nutrients created artificially in a pure and easy-to-use form. These are sold as either dry granules, water-soluble crystals, or liquid concentrate. You'll also find various types of compressed pellets and other unique forms of slow-release fertilizer that are designed for specific uses.

Dry granules are the most common form of fertilizer, because they can be easily packaged and don't have to be mixed up or specially prepared. BEST Turf

Supreme is one of the most widely known brands for the lawn, and there are generic equivalents to BEST that are less expensive. Other all-purpose formulas, such as 16–16–16, are more universal and can be used on everything in the garden. This granulated lawn and all-purpose fertilizer must be watered well to dissolve the granules into the soil before plants can use the nutrients.

The most widely advertised brand of water-soluble crystals is Miracle-Gro, which is applied with a garden-hose proportioning device that eliminates the need for mixing it up in a watering can. Liquid concentrate such as Liquinox is also mixed with water using a proportioning device or the watering can.

All name-brand manufacturers of fertilizer advertise widely, which costs money, and this overhead is passed on to you. Stick with generics whenever possible and you'll save a bundle, as long as you read the contents label carefully.

TIGHTWAD GARDENING TIP: There are newer fertilizers that contain weed killers designed to cut down on labor. Weeds are automatically treated as you fertilize the lawn, which is a great convenience, but these newer products cost a lot more than normal untreated fertilizers. For those who face crabgrass invasions in the lawn, a weed-killer fertilizer product is a good buy, as it eliminates the need to purchase herbicide. Since getting this type of grass out of a lawn can be a nightmare and frequently the grass comes back, it's worth the extra cost to control unwanted weeds, particularly when busy lifestyles leave a limited amount of time for lawn care.

PEST-CONTROL PRODUCTS

In the past, pest-control products were primarily agricultural chemicals packaged in small quantities. Most people can't even pronounce the technical names for the active ingredients, so they are sold under a trade name. Their prominence in the marketplace is slipping because of some bad press, which spreads paranoia and

TIGHTWAD GARDENING TIP: It is important to know when to spray plants. If you spray in the sun or just before sun reaches the garden, the spray will intensify the sunshine and cause burning. This is particularly important when using oil sprays.

- Whenever a recipe calls for dish soap, ammonia, or other household products, don't use any with special additives such as fragrances or sudsing agents. Those sold in health-food stores are the most reliable and consist of more organic detergents than the name brands do.
- Ivory dish soap is favored by golf course greenskeepers as a mild solution to wash oils off the grass.
- When using bleach, stick with Clorox or Purex, as other brands may have altered formulas less suitable for plants.
- When spraying plants, be sure to treat the undersides of the leaves, where many insects tend to hide, and when you treat fungi, it is essential to be thorough, or untreated remnants will reinfect the plants.

mistrust of this heavily regulated industry. Yet those who have suffered from persistent infestations of insects know that nothing short of toxic warfare will make their homes and gardens habitable.

The following recipes have been collected from different sources, some old and some new. As any experienced gardener knows, what works in one state or climate doesn't necessarily work in another.

Before you spend money on any pest-control products, consider making your own. You may have all the components you need right in the kitchen to creat a batch of highly effective bug sauce. In addition, you can rest assured that nothing toxic is used in your garden. Test the recipe on a small portion of the plant before subjecting the whole thing to a new concoction. Wait forty-eight hours before the second application to the remainder of the plant. Also keep in mind that salt has been used as a weed killer, but it can render the soil too alkaline for many other desirable plants. To see how serious this can be, simply study the devastation of plants along roadsides in snow country where rock salt has been used extensively to melt ice on pavement.

BUG SAUCE

- Insecticidal soap: Mix 4 tablespoons of liquid dish soap into 1 gallon of water, then spray on plants. Kills **aphids, spider mites, and many other insect pests**.
- To control **black flies,** add 1 tablespoon plain ammonia to a quart of water and pour into soil.
- Spray leaves to control **white flies** with a combination of 2 tablespoons of liquid dishwashing detergent and a gallon of water. You can also vacuum them up with a Dustbuster held a few inches away from plant leaves.
- Marigolds are planted in vegetable gardens because they repel soil-borne **nematodes** that infect plant roots. Distribute marigolds throughout the garden for more widespread protection.
- Pepper spray is made by combining long, red cayenne peppers with water in a blender. You'll find inexpensive dried peppers in the Mexican spice section of the supermarket. They're said to control **ants, spiders, cabbage worms, caterpillars, and tomato hornworms**. Add pureed garlic or onion to control a broader spectrum of pests. Try sprinkling ground dried cayenne peppers into **anthills** to evict the entire nest.
- **Red spider mites** can be controlled with a spray of leftover coffee.

FERTILIZERS

Ethel's Elixir: Ethel Young, a California Master Gardener, has a special concoction she uses with great success. Whether or not it is less expensive than commercial-based products is difficult to tell, but it is nontoxic and completely safe on food crops. Combine in a gallon jug:

$1/4$ cup Epsom salts	$1/4$ cup baking powder
$1/4$ cup rubbing alcohol	$1/4$ cup plain ammonia
1 8-ounce can of beer	6 aspirin

Add water to fill jug. Stir or shake to dissolve aspirin. Spray leaves or drench soil around base of plant.

WEED KILLERS

Weeds growing in paving cracks: Pour boiling water with a few tablespoons of salt added. To prevent new sprouts, sprinkle salt in the crack, just as the Romans sowed salt into the Carthaginians' fields so the earth would bear no crops. Beware of overdoing, as the salt may dissolve with rainwater and harm other plants nearby, particularly species that prefer acidic soil.

FUNGICIDE

For mildew, black spot, or rust, mix 3 teaspoons baking soda and 1 teaspoon liquid dish soap into 1 gallon water and spray plants.

OTHER STUFF

- **Deer Repellent:** Mix 1 egg white with a blender container full of water and blend on low speed. Spray mixture on plant. Repeat after rain or as needed.
- **Deer or Pet Repellent:** Mix cayenne pepper with water in a blender. Spray on plants. Also works for other animals and pets that chew plants.
- **Slugs:** Pour some beer into a tin pie pan and place it out in the garden. Slugs and snails can't resist the yeast and get trapped in the pan. You can intensify the attractiveness of this bait by adding a pinch of brewer's yeast.
- **Climbing Pests** that must crawl up tree trunks to complete their life cycles can be stopped with a sticky ring of molasses painted in a ring around the trunk a few feet from the bottom. The pests become bogged down in the molasses, which breaks their reproductive ability. Reapply the molasses when it dries out and loses its stickiness, or gets washed off by rain.

The movement toward least-toxic pest control has placed a good number of new products on the market to compete with the old chemical standbys. Now, not only do you have to recognize the chemicals, you must negotiate the barrage of new organic products as well. Here we find another example of how marketing costs us more for less product. Canned fruit with added sugar in the syrup costs *less* than fruit canned without sugar. Likewise, a bottle of insecticidal soap, which is basically just water and detergent, can cost more than a chemical product that is far more difficult to manufacture. In both cases we are paying for the newer, sometimes more "politically correct" choice—the manufacturers are quick to exploit our consciences.

To simplify this aspect of garden supply, try to avoid purchasing any of these products unless you have no other choice. Disposal problems develop when you buy a bottle of concentrated pesticide, because you may use it just once or twice, then find yourself stuck with the remainder, which is potent toxic waste that shouldn't be thrown out like everything else. Not to mention the fact that it's a waste of money to pay for so much (unused) product.

Problems with insects often go away on their own, or you can simply wash the pests away with a strong jet of water. Your local farm adviser will have free or low-cost pest-control literature that is in keeping with less chemically dependent integrated pest management. IPM is neither all-chemical nor all-organic but seeks the most effective control measures without overkill. You can also buy one of the many pest-control books on the market. *Tiny Game Hunting*, by Hilary Dole Llein and Adrian M. Wenner, provides all the details you need regarding pest control and the least toxic process.

BEER BUDGET ITEMS: If you live in the country or have a large home-site, the home-improvement store is not always the place to get the best price for fertilizer or seeds when you are looking at application rates of 250 pounds per acre or more. Many communities have agricultural supply sources for growers, farmers, and city public works departments that need to obtain large quantities of fertilizers and seed. You should know exactly what you need and how much is required before you price these bulk supplies. You may even need a truck to pick up the materials, although some companies will deliver. To avoid spoilage, be sure you have a clean, dry place to store the materials until you are ready to use them.

SOME TIPS ON PEST-CONTROL STUFF
YOU HAVE AROUND THE HOUSE

Snail, slugs, and caterpillars have a difficult time crawling over sharp, granulated materials such as diatomaceous earth. You have to buy garden-variety diatomaceous earth to use this nontoxic method of control, but virtually any abrasive surface can be used as a barrier. Consider common sandpaper that is manufactured in sheets, belts, and disks for various types of power tools; even used sandpaper can be effective. Sandpaper rings with a hole cut in the center can be laid upon the soil around seedlings as a barrier, or you can also cut the disk into two halves. It's nearly impossible for these hungry pests to reach young plants without crossing over. If you don't have enough used sandpaper, go to the nearest cabinetmaker or high-school wood shop. Auto body shops also go through a lot of sandpaper. If you ask, they'll be glad to give you what they have on hand and save their used sheets in the future.

CHAPTER 2

ECONOMICAL SOIL IMPROVEMENT

Successful gardeners spend a lot of time improving the soil both before and after planting. This is because plants consume nutrients that exist in the soil, and unless the nutrients are replaced through fertilizers, a deficiency results. Without nutrients, plants simply won't grow. When organic matter is worked into the soil to make it lighter, microorganisms in the soil begin the decomposition process, which transforms it into humus, a form most easily used by plants. But eventually it disappears too. One of the ongoing activities of good gardening, particularly in intensively cultivated areas such as vegetable plots and flowerbeds, is the enrichment of the soil.

FERTILIZERS, SOIL AMENDMENTS, AND MULCHES

An ideal material might serve more than one of these purposes at a time.

There are often misunderstandings about the nutrient levels of various organic soil-improving materials. The following table lists most organic sources of nutrients and humus, allowing you to make comparisons. For example, a pound of steer manure, which contains 2 percent nitrogen, has a greater nutrient value by weight than horse manure, with only 0.7 percent nitrogen. Many of these materials are by-products of agriculture and the food industry that have fallen out of use in recent

or three trips. Be sure to tie a tarp or heavy blanket over the load to prevent hazards to motorists behind you.

One thing to consider is how you'll get the material into your trailer, a problem beginner gardeners often overlook. Filling a trailer by hand can be both time-consuming and labor-intensive. Some farmers keep a tractor handy to clean out their barns and move the manure. This is ideal for loading up your order, so it's worthwhile to ask the farmer ahead of time if he can help you out with the tractor. If no loader is available, bring broad, flat shovels and be prepared to go to work. For bulky lightweight materials, a deep snow-scooping shovel or a pitchfork is perfect.

Liquid products, such as tankage, are a bit complicated to load and haul. They can't be dumped straight into a truck or trailer, so if you're determined to harvest this resource, you'll have to use 50-gallon drums. Beware: A drum of this size filled with any sort of liquid can be *very* heavy to move and isn't a realistic choice for many people. You can obtain drums from junkyards or industrial companies that use oil or other liquid products in quantity, although residual product still inside the drum can contaminate the liquid you plan to move, so be sure it is clean. If it's not, try using a steam cleaner at a do-it-yourself car wash.

These drums may have an open top, or be completely sealed with only a small

....

TIGHTWAD GARDENING TIP: Woody organic matter such as straw or wood shavings that have not decomposed are excellent for breaking up heavy soils. But when soil microorganisms try to break this material down, they require nitrogen for the job, so any manure or other nitrogen sources added with the woody stuff will be consumed in the decomposition process. If the woody stuff is added without any nitrogen source at all, the microorganisms will rob the surrounding soil of what nitrogen exists there, leaving the soil *less fertile* than when you started. To compensate, you can add some commercial granular nitrogen fertilizer (lawn formulas are best) when working with woody organic matter in order to maintain or increase nutrient levels.

....

hole. The covered drums are more difficult to fill but easier to transport, because stops and starts in transit may cause the liquid in open drums to slosh around and spill over. Once at home, you can store the liquid in the drum and use it as needed.

THE MANURE SAFARI

Manure is sold in various forms, sometimes pure, sometimes mixed with livestock bedding, such as shavings or straw. Pure product is the most potent in terms of nutrients, but when mixed with bedding the manure contains both nutrients and soil amendments.

In some cases the only reasonable way to obtain manure is to buy it by the bag from your local home-improvement store. To buy at the best prices, wait until the store is offering a promotion. Look for notices in the newspaper advertising inserts and junk mailers. These stores use steer manure as a lure by advertising it at incredibly low prices, such as 50 cents a bag, because they know you'll probably buy a lot of other things you hadn't planned on. But stick with your goal and stock up with as many bags as you can manage while the sale is on.

Bagged poultry manure, along with other animal waste, rarely contains bedding materials. It is usually sterilized and composted, so there is little risk of burning or importing weed seeds. The problem is that not only do you have to add bedding, you'll also have to buy 5,000 bags to get a good-sized job done, and because this wonderful humus is prime rib to soil microbes, you'll probably have to add the same amount each year after it decomposes. One good trailer load of stockyard manure with either sand, straw, or shavings bedding is worth more than bagged material, because you get some amendments in there, too.

So where to begin your manure safari? The most obvious sources are dairy farms, but there are many smaller-scale beef cattle operations on the outskirts of the suburbs. Chicken farms, egg ranches, hog farms, sheep operations, and goat dairies are all excellent sources of clean manure. Sometimes health-food stores buy milk and cheese directly from organic goat dairies, or range-fed eggs, so they might be a good connection. To find these elusive folks, contact feed stores, as they supply everyone with grain and animal-care products. Many livestock ranchers are relieved if you call requesting manure, since it tends to accumulate, and on small farms disposal can become a serious problem. In most cases you should be able to obtain it free of charge, and with luck there will be a tractor loader available.

Every police officer who rides a horse stables it for the night somewhere, as do the drivers of horses that pull buggies around city parks, so stop to inquire from the driver about the barn location. Stables and private equestrian country clubs are all good sources for free manure. Tack and saddle stores know larger equestrian operations such as racetracks. Don't forget large-animal veterinarians, who are intimate with livestock owners.

Colleges and universities with agriculture or veterinary programs usually have livestock on campus or at nearby sites where the students learn to care for animals. In some cases you'll not only find cattle, but horses, sheep, goats, and even poultry. Since these are public institutions, access is not difficult. You may even be able to bribe students to help you shovel. On a smaller scale, high schools and grammar schools have classroom animals such as rabbits. If you provide a container, they may be willing to dump the unwanted contents of cages for you to pick up.

CHEAP-SCAPES CHOICES: Even in the city there are hidden sources of manures. Many urban dwellers raise pigeons on the rooftops of apartment buildings. If you know of any, take a hike up there with a sturdy bucket, preferably with a lid. Help the bird lover clean out his or her cages and reap this ever-so-fertile harvest. The manure is usually too fresh to use directly in the garden, but it makes a great booster to a compost pile, straw pile, or leaf-mold bin.

Pet stores tend to accumulate quite a bit of manure of different types that must be discarded, and it's often mixed with shavings or other types of bedding. You can encourage them to collect it for you by supplying a container. As a general rule, manures from meat-eating animals are undesirable, so be sure to state your preferences. Stick with waste from birds, rabbits, guinea pigs, rats, and mice.

If you're willing to get into some exotic-animal manures, contact the zoo or wild-animal parks nearby. You have no idea how much manure one elephant generates after consuming its 500 pounds of plant material *every day!* In fact, elephant manure is perfect for heavy soils because it is rich in woody materials. A final source of manure is the dog pound or humane society. Though you can't use dog or cat waste, since they eat meat, such organizations sometimes take in barnyard animals as well.

CHECKLIST FOR MANURE SOURCES

Cow dairy farm

Goat dairy farm

Horse stables

Pet stores

Exotic-bird breeders

Slaughterhouse stockyards

Wild-animal parks or petting zoos

College/university agriculture schools

High school/grammar school classroom animals

Chicken or egg ranches

Sheep ranches

Racetrack

Zoo

Humane society

Veterinarian

AGRICULTURAL BY-PRODUCTS

Most people don't realize that after a crop is harvested it doesn't go straight to the supermarket. Many crops must undergo extensive processing in order to become market-ready, and often there are by-products that result. Because the crops originate with plants, the by-products are primarily organic matter. Some of these products are in high demand and turned over to other manufacturers, who further process or bag them for sale.

The key is knowing which by-products originate from which crops, and which crops are grown in your state or county. In some cases farmers or processing plants will charge a very small fee or nothing at all for their by-product, depending on demand and whether you pick it up yourself. This need not be drudgery. A trip to the country towing a trailer in search of agricultural by-products can become a fun family outing or an opportunity for a picnic after the work is done.

HULLS AND SHELLS

The nutritious grains of crops such as rice, buckwheat, and oats are encased in thin, fibrous hulls. After harvesting, the grains are processed and the hulls removed. Rice hulls are one of the great undiscovered soil amendments, because they resist decomposition, are lightweight, and are finely textured. To find a cheap or free source of hulls, contact the nearest agricultural office for your state or county and inquire about farmers growing one of these grains in the area. If they are growing nearby, ask about farmers' cooperatives or processing plants, because these are where you'll find the by-products stockpiled. Because *dry* hulls are so lightweight, you can pack them into a truck or trailer and transport a huge quantity in one load.

Nut shells or hulls are also valuable because they are typically hard and durable. Because shells are heavy, they make both functional and decorative mulches depending on the nut type. Ground walnut shells are in high demand today because of their density, uniformity of color, and resistance to decomposition. Pecan shells, widely available in the Southern states, are similar to walnuts. Almonds and peanuts have more fibrous shells, which can serve as either mulch or soil amendments. Packing houses that can fruits like peaches or cherries leave an abundance of pits, which, when crushed, can be of considerable value for soil improvement.

POMACE

This is a term given to the residues of olives, fruits, and grapes after processing at either packing houses or wineries. Pomace consists of skins and seed fragments that contain only scant quantities of nutrients, but the seed makes a good soil amendment or addition to compost piles. It is not as "clean" as hulls or shells, but it is usually free for the asking. Cotton-gin waste is another product of the Southern states and the West. Like hulls, it contains very little nutrition but if obtained cheaply enough it makes a worthwhile addition to compost or manure. To find these by-products, contact the state or county department of agriculture and ask for the names of driers and packing houses. If wineries exist in the area, they will be listed in your Yellow Pages or with the chamber of commerce.

STRAW

Straw or oat hay is inexpensive and easy to buy, since it is packed neatly into bales.

You can buy hay from any feed store, and the bale should fit at least partway into the trunk of most passenger cars. Wheat or rice straw is most common but contains very little nutrition. Bean straw and shredded cornstalks are also useful and can sometimes be found in agricultural communities. Wheat straw also contains occasional grain heads with a few seeds attached, and when watered, these often sprout into full-fledged wheat. Let these plants mature and dry into free bonus material for crafts and flower arrangements during autumn, or for decorating Christmas packages.

Straw is popular with vegetable gardeners as a surface mulch that can be tilled back into the soil at the end of the season after it has begun to decompose. It is also the cheapest material available for controlling soil erosion on newly graded slopes. In some cases straw is actually pushed into moist ground with a shovel in order to anchor it and provide a stable bench for seeds to lodge and germinate. If used as an ornamental mulch, the straw should be ground up or shredded into smaller pieces. This is where your investment in a chipper/shredder machine really pays off. But as with any other type of woody material, you must add some nitrogen fertilizer to aid the decomposition process by soil microbes.

Since straw is so easy to get, you can stockpile it to decompose in a forgotten corner of the garden. The result will surprise you. Two bales of compressed straw create quite a bit of organic matter and are a good way to begin a lazy gardener's compost pile. Simply cut the wires and separate the flakes. Tear each flake apart and fluff the straw up into a big pile. Then jump on it (kids love this) to compact it a bit, and water the whole thing. If you do this in the fall, winter rains will take care of keeping the pile moist.

Occasionally add handfuls of fertilizer high in nitrogen to the pile, along with manure, leaves, or anything else you have on hand, to introduce microorganisms. Prepared "compost maker" additives are suitable but can be costly. Keep the pile wet so the straw rots more quickly, and forget it for a year or more. The result is not as beautiful as compost, but the fibrous material in straw makes it a wonderful amendment for clay soil.

Another method of improving an entire vegetable garden plot in cold climates is literally to cover the whole thing with a layer of fluffed-up straw in fall. Make the layer a foot or so deep. In fact, breaking the bales and tearing them apart for this purpose is a terrific game for kids. They get to throw it around and then stomp it down afterward. Over winter the entire mass will be subjected to snow and rain, which causes the straw to rot. By spring you should have a condensed layer of mulch alive with organisms that can be cultivated back into the soil at great benefit to overall fertility.

In some climates the straw may not decompose enough by spring and will bind up in your rototiller tines. If you have a strong rotary lawn mower, remove the catcher bag and simply run it over the straw right after you spread it out. The straw should be very dry so that the mower can chop up the stems into fragments that will decompose more easily and till well come spring.

Some gardeners have gone so far as to make straw bales into planters for vegetable root crops such as carrots and radishes. Place the bale, still bound by its wires, in a location that is *poorly drained*. Water your bale frequently and pile some manure or topsoil on top so it can gradually work into the straw as you water. A few chops or punctures here and there help too. Keep in mind that as the center of the bale decomposes it will generate heat, providing bottom heat for seedlings, which speeds germination. This also helps extend your growing season in cold-weather climates.

When the straw on the top of the bale decomposes enough to allow you to tear it into pieces, loosen it enough to plant the first season's crop of beans or summer squash. These plants quickly send out large root systems into the center of the bale, loosening straw deeper down. The second year you can try root crops, and depending on your climate you may be able to plant into the bale for three years running, or until it has disintegrated too far to hold plants. At that time just cut the wires and use the now highly fertile organic matter in the rest of your garden.

COVER CROPS AND GREEN MANURE

For centuries farmers planted their fields in winter with temporary cover crops of leguminous plants. These include many different strains of clovers, alfalfa, and peas. Legumes have the unique ability to take nitrogen out of the air and put it into the soil, unlike all other plants, which take nitrogen out of the soil. When legumi-

COMMON COVER CROPS

Alfalfa, acyceclover, alsike clover, Austrian winter pea, beggarweed, berseem, bur clover, cowpea, crimson clover, hairy indigo, lespedeza, lupine, persian clover, red clover, roughpea, sesbania, sourclover, soybeans, sweetclover, velvetbeans, vetch, wood's clover.

nous plants die, there is still a lot of nitrogen trapped in their bodies. Then, when they are tilled in at the end of the season, the soil gets a second boost of nitrogen. This process produces "green manure."

We can also benefit from cover crops and green manure in vegetable gardens. You can sow in the fall to prepare for a spring garden, or if you aren't growing a summer garden, sow in early spring. You can do this every year if you wish. It's also a great quick fix to improve the fallow ground of a new homesite and control surface erosion at the same time. If you plant in the fall, there will be sufficient rainfall to support the cover crop. Sowing in spring is more difficult in dry climates and may require irrigation.

Look in the Yellow Pages for feed stores or farm-supply stores, which usually carry cover-crop leguminous seed in bulk at a very low price. They will also know which crops will grow best in your climate. Seeding rates will be expressed in pounds per 1,000 square feet or pounds per acre.

Planting cover crops isn't always possible, but there's a way to take advantage of the second nitrogen boost using baled alfalfa. Refer to the table on page 18, which details nutrient contents of organic materials. Compare the nutrient levels of alfalfa hay with manure, and you'll be surprised at how similar they are. Alfalfa is sold in compressed bales that are easy to transport and relatively inexpensive. If you spread the alfalfa in a layer over your veggie garden in the fall, it will decompose and release nitrogen into the soil. Running a lawn mower over it while it's still dry will chop up the alfalfa straw into manageable fragments. This technique is worth its weight in gold considering the amount of organic matter and nutrients you get per bale coupled with the low cost and ease of transportation.

For years some gardeners have raved about the results of mulching ornamental plants with alfalfa-pellet livestock feed, which works on the same green-manure principle. Pellets are simply bale alfalfa chopped up and compressed into a more manageable form for use on roses and other landscape plants. Distribute them around the base of a plant, and in a short time they disintegrate into the soil, offering both nitrogen and organic matter. Pellets are a great alternative for urban gardeners because they are sold in neatly sealed bags, but the processing and packaging drive the price much higher than that of baled alfalfa.

FOREST BY-PRODUCTS

With recent slowdowns in the logging industry, our ability to use forest by-products is becoming more limited and expensive. The landscape industry uses ground bark of various conifers as a decorative mulch because of its uniform color and texture. A good alternative is wood chips generated by tree-trimming companies. Most of them reduce the volume of their waste with portable commercial chippers. Once their truck is full of the chips, they have to dump it somewhere or pay expensive landfill fees. If you make arrangements to have it dumped in your driveway, you'll enjoy a lifetime supply for all your gardening needs. But be prepared for a big pile, since they must dump the entire load.

WARNING: If you don't know the source of a wood-chip supply, be careful how you handle it. Sometimes poison oak or poison sumac is mixed in, and the residual oil in the wood can cause serious rashes. Also beware of thorny chips from plants such as roses or berry vines. When concentrated, very oily chips from trees like eucalyptus, black walnut, and camphor can actually discourage plant growth because of certain chemicals in these plants.

Wood chips can be obtained from many sources. Consult the tree-trimming section of your Yellow Pages for local companies that can supply you with chips. Even if they charge you a small fee, it's worth the price compared with what it costs for similar materials at a garden center. And the fact that you don't have to haul it yourself is worth a few extra bucks. Some city or county public-works departments chip the prunings of city trees on streets, parks, and open space. They may have a stockpile in their corporation yard or will deliver a load to you after their next job.

Other sources of wood chips include the U.S. Forest Service, reclamation districts, and highway departments.

If you see tree trimming or brush clearing going on in your area, don't hesitate to stop and ask if the workers will dump their load at your house. If you dangle a six-pack, a twenty-dollar bill, or hot coffee under their noses, chances are they'll be especially willing to help you out.

In some areas landfills are separating organic materials from the regular garbage. There may be an organic-matter recycling effort going on near your home, or you can start one in which leaves, chips, clippings, and other types of fine garden refuse are stockpiled at the dump. Residents can support the program by paying a small fee to access this great garden-making stuff at the dump site.

CHEAP-SCAPES CHOICES: There are two household by-products that can go straight into the gardens. Used coffee grounds contain fairly high amounts of nitrogen, and because thay are finely ground will mix easily into garden soil. Wood ash from the fireplace or barbecue contains some phosphorus and potassium. Many people add it to their soils or spread it thinly beneath fruit trees. Snails and other creepy crawlers won't pass over fresh wood ash, so it makes a good barrier protection for plants. But the real value to soil is the small chunks of charcoal mixed with the ash, which can be worked into heavy soil as an amendment to improve drainage. Beware of concentrating too much ash in one place, because it can be caustic.

Sawdust is also a valuable soil amendment and a great addition to compost piles. You can buy shavings in tightly packed bales, but avoid cedar shavings, as these are far more expensive than the standard "livestock bedding" you find at the feed store. Free shavings or sawdust are fairly easy to obtain. Again, there is the problem of loading and hauling, but since this material is lightweight you can use heavy-duty yard and garbage bags to get it home in the trunk of your car.

High school wood shops are great untapped resources, because every day the

UNEXPECTED CHEAP OR FREE FERTILIZERS

Iron: If your plants become chlorotic (their leaves turn yellow while the veins remain green), they may be suffering from iron deficiency. Don't panic, because a cost-free supplement is at your fingertips. Old-time farmers used to gather up pieces of scrap iron such as wire, tin cans, or virtually anything that rusts and throw them into a bucket of water. When you have a good "rust tea," add a quarter cup to a gallon of fresh water and pour on your chlorotic plants.

Fisherman's Fertilizer: Ever wonder where to discard the innards, heads, and tails when cleaning fish? Just bury them in the garden at least 8 inches deep so cats won't be lured by odors. Then allow at least a year for decomposition before you plant in the newly enriched soil. Kind of a poor man's fish emulsion.

Eggshells: Most vegetable gardens and annual flowerbeds can use calcium. Eggshells contain generous amounts of calcium, and they don't break down very quickly. Instead of throwing them out, crush the shells, rinse the fragments with water, then cultivate them into soil for a free, organic calcium supplement that thinks it's a soil amendment.

Sulfur Supplements: A sulfur deficiency in your soil will cause the leaves of new growth to turn yellow. To remedy the problem, simply cut the heads off matches and work the sulfured ends into the soil. If the green color returns to the new growth, you can be sure a lack of sulfur was the problem.

shop is swept up and the wood by-products discarded. Contact the shop teacher to find out how and when to gather up the shavings. Other options are cabinetmakers, wood-turning operations, or wood sculptors. Consider lumberyards, because some of them cut their wood products to size for customers. Even firewood lots may have shavings, along with tons of bark fragments you can also use as a surface mulch. Just wander in and chat with their saw man, and don't hesitate to strike a bargain.

COMPOST AND LEAF MOLD

Much of what goes down your garbage disposal or into the garbage can be recycled into one of the most beneficial soil-improvement materials available. Best of all, it's absolutely free. Just as you recycle paper, glass, and aluminum, compost recycles organic wastes from the kitchen. Compost is decomposed organic matter that is high in nutrients and makes an excellent soil conditioner. But it takes a tremendous amount of compost to support a garden of any size, and because in some climates it can take up to a year for the waste to decompose, you're looking at a time investment too.

MAKING A COMPOST BIN

You may have already encountered one of the many compost-making containers advertised in magazines or on TV. There are two ways to look at these products. On the one hand, some people aren't avid gardeners and compost kitchen refuse for ecological reasons. These folks enjoy the convenience and small scale of these composting products. Most are containers designed so that finished compost can be removed from the bottom, eliminating the need to stir up the material for more even decomposition.

On the other hand, people who are avid gardeners view their compost as a major commodity needed to improve soil throughout the landscape. Considering how much compost is needed to fortify the soil of a 10-by-10-foot veggie plot, most commercial compost bins or drums produce very little product. For the frugal gardener, a much bigger compost bin is required.

By far the cheapest and oldest method of composting is simply to pile up your materials as farmers traditionally have. But for people with city yards these heaps spread out too much, becoming messy and difficult to turn. An enclosure or bin helps keep the compost contained and speeds up the decomposition process. Ideally a compost bin should be no more than 3 to 5 feet deep, but may vary in size depending on how much material you expect to have, and the amount of space available. The average is about 4 by 6 feet.

In order to get the entire mass of compost to decompose, you'll have to turn it now and then to get the surface material down deeper, where there is more microorganism activity. You can simply mix up the pile, but this can be difficult when you are constrained to a single bin. The solution is to build two bins side by side that share a center wall. Once the first bin is full, fork it over into the second bin.

What was on the top of the pile in bin #1 ends up at the bottom of bin #2.

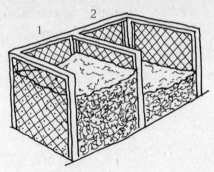

LEFT: *This simple two-bin compost pile is easy to build. Create a framework of two-by-fours, then staple fine-mesh chicken wire or similar material to the frame. A two-bin system allows you to fork the contents of one bin into the other, an easier way to turn compost than simply stirring up a single pile.* CENTER: *It's easy to create a compost pile by simply layering house and garden refuse as it becomes available. You can shake in compost-building products or fertilizers to enrich the mix. Remember, if the pile is too wet, it ferments, and if it is too dry, no decomposition will occur.* RIGHT: *You can use woven-wire field fencing to create a leaf-mold corral or a single-bin compost pile. The enclosure can be as large or small as you wish, because often space is the single most important factor when you are sizing this kind of enclosure.*

The cheapest enclosure, which is not pretty but works quite well, uses woven wire fencing. The best place to get small segments of this stuff cheap or free is from fencing contractors (you'll find them listed under this heading in the Yellow Pages). Before erecting a new fence, these companies often take down an old one. Their waste product may be perfect for your compost bin. Chain-link fencing is ideal, since it is durable, galvanized, and very stiff and has smaller holes than field fencing. The only drawback is that you need bolt cutters because the wire is so thick. Woven-wire field fencing is used for livestock—the openings vary from 1 inch or so to as much as 6 inches. Chicken wire is also a good choice. Welded wire mesh is used for reinforcing concrete slabs; it too can be reused, and it tends to be much stiffer than the woven types. See a concrete contractor for scraps of welded mesh.

Smaller holes in your wire enclosure help prevent the organic matter from working through during the composting process. If you're stuck with big mesh wire, simply build the bin with a double layer of wire, or line the inside with plastic or wood.

You can anchor the corners of your compost bin with scrap lumber such as 4-by-4-inch posts, though these will eventually rot out. You'll have to dig post holes to set these solidly in place. Another option is to use segments of old galvanized pipe at least 1 inch in diameter. If the soil is moist, you can avoid digging post holes by simply pounding these in with a sledgehammer. Yet another option is metal "T" fenceposts used by ranchers with field fencing. They run about $2 apiece at a farm-supply, home-improvement, or hardware store. Attached to one end of these posts is a fin that stabilizes them in the soil. A note of caution: "T" posts can be impossible to use in rocky ground. If you have unusually difficult soil, you may have to wait until after a good rain to pound in your posts.

For more ambitious gardeners with a few bucks to spend, the most durable compost bins are made of concrete blocks, bricks, or railroad ties. Masonry is not only expensive to buy, but if you don't lay it yourself there will be a mason to pay. Railroad ties are probably the most widely used material for building permanent compost bins, because they stack well, can be interlocked at the corners, and are resistant to decay because of creosote treatments. Railroad ties can be easily held in place with pipe, reinforcement bar, or "T" posts. Many gardeners may have a problem with the creosote, as it may leach chemicals into the compost, although leaching is minimal.

How to Make Compost

When a compost pile is functioning properly, it becomes the breeding ground for important bacteria and other microorganisms that feed off organic matter and turn it into a crumbly, nutrient-rich humus. Rapid decomposition will cause the center of the pile to reach temperatures around 180° F., which is hot enough to sterilize weed seeds. While the center is heated by activity, the top, bottom, and sides are cool and resist decomposition. When the pile is stirred up or turned, this places material (that was once on the outside) at the interior, where it too begins decomposing.

Just how often you mix or turn this stuff depends on your region, the time of year, and average temperatures. In warm weather (which may be all year round in Florida), turn your compost every 2 or 3 months or even more frequently. In cooler climates, twice a year may be adequate. Some plant fibers resist decomposition more than others, so to speed them up add some fertilizer, either granular commercial products or just a layer of manure.

When you add to the compost pile, pack down new deposits until they form a 6-inch layer. Then sprinkle fertilizer on top and water thoroughly. It's also helpful to add topsoil between the layers to introduce soil-borne organisms, which help speed up the process. Avoid letting your compost pile become too wet, as this drowns the microorganisms, and if it is too dry, they lack sufficient moisture to remain alive. Push a broom handle or a piece of pipe into the center of the pile now and then to make aeration holes that provide oxygen for the microorganisms in between the times when you turn the entire mass.

If your compost pile doesn't heat up as it should, dig a test hole into the center and check the moisture content. Beware of any black, slimy material that emits a rotten, offensive odor. This means the pile is oversaturated with water and *fermenting* due to lack of oxygen. Proper decomposition requires plenty of oxygen, so you'd better open it up right away. If the materials are cool and dry, dampen but do not soak the pile. If you've added too much green leafy stuff, such as grass clippings, the pile may start smelling like ammonia. To offset this, work some dry shavings or leaves into the pile.

Composting is not a quick process, nor is it an exact science. The rate of decomposition doubles for every 18-degree rise in air temperature, so it occurs much more quickly in the summer months. The average pile will take about six months in warm climates and up to two years in the far north.

Waste into Wealth—What to Put into Your Compost Pile and What Not To

It would be much more efficient if kitchen garbage disposals dumped their chewed-up contents directly into our compost piles, but not all refuse can be composted, as the table on page 34 indicates.

It's tough to separate animal products from everything else. The next best thing is to throw your kitchen scraps into the blender or food processor to chop them up *before* adding them to your compost pile. Although they can go into the heap whole, chopping makes them decompose a lot faster. Anything from house or garden that is waste plant material makes good compost as long as it is no thicker than a pencil.

GOOD AND BAD STUFF FOR THE COMPOST PILE

Woody materials decompose more slowly than other stuff. Make sure these and all other components of the compost pile are finely ground up before being added. Add extra manure or fertilizer to compensate for an overabundance of woody material and to encourage more rapid decompostion.

Good Stuff	Bad Stuff
Autumn leaves from deciduous trees	No oak, holly, or conifer leaves—these are acidic and more resistant to decay.
Dead annuals and perennials	Toxic plants: eucalyptus, poison oak, poison sumac, black walnut
Pruning twigs cut short (less than a pencil in diameter)	No plants with thorns: roses, berry vines
Workshop sawdust or shavings (Woody—add extra fertilizer.)	No wood by-products from lumber treated with wood-preservative chemicals
Fireplace ashes (Don't overdo it.)	Metals—they rust; plastics—do not decompose; glass—sharp edges.
Lawn clippings (Cause ammonia—spread and dry out first.)	Aggressive weeds such as Bermuda, which sprout from runners and roots
Vacuum-cleaner dust (Without pet hairs)	Bones, hair, meat, grease, and other animal products
Leguminous plants of the pea family that add nitrogen to the soil and compost: clover, pea vines, etc.	Any plants, plant parts, or soils that show signs of disease, pests, or undesirable webby mycelia of soil fungi
Vegetable leftovers from kitchen. Coffee grounds, tea leaves, pasta, and bread. Crush and rinse eggshells before using.	Toxic substances such as oil, paint, or cleaning products
Finely shredded brown paper bags, cardboard, and newspapers	

There are all kinds of other cheap or free stuff you can add to the compost pile to enlarge it and speed the decomposition process. Earthworms, especially night crawlers, can be salvaged from your garden and set free in your compost pile. If you know an avid fisherman, he or she may fish with worms, and at the end of the day the little squirmers still in the bait container can be recycled into your compost pile.

TIGHTWAD GARDENING TIP: There are good reasons for keeping animal products out of the compost pile. The biggest problem is that when they decay, the smell draws in varmints from all corners of the globe—neighborhood dogs and cats, hungry coyotes, and other wildlife. In some cases harmful bacteria can breed upon animal products in a compost pile as well. The bad reputation of compost piles is from these types of additives and their odors, which tend to turn off neighbors to the practice altogether. Even if you avoid animal products, its better to locate your compost bin away from neighbors' outdoor living spaces, so there will be no "bone" of contention between you. To be safe, stick with organic plant matter.

Some avid composters advocate limited amounts of urine as a good addition to the pile. Urine contains from 10 to 15 percent nitrogen plus other goodies that speed up microorganism activity. The downside is it can create an odor problem if added too frequently. Use your own judgment on this.

Fast and Free Leaf Mold

Leaf mold is "lazy gardener's compost," because it is easy to make and ready to use far sooner than compost. It does not contain the high nutrient content of compost, but it is a fine soil improver that can be enhanced when used with commercial fertilizers. Leaves are plentiful in autumn and are either sent to the landfill in bags, burned, or shredded into mulch if you are fortunate enough to have a chipper/shredder machine. But most of us aren't so lucky and have to make leaf mold the old-fashioned way.

You should not be limited to the leaves that fall from your own trees. Chances are, everyone in your neighborhood is doing the same thing, raking and more raking. If you notify them you want the leaves that they bag for the garbage truck, they will probably agree to reserve these autumn presents for you. Imagine how much of our fall organic matter harvest gets thrown out!

Follow these instructions during fall, and by summer you should have an ideal soil conditioner or quality mulching material.

1. Obtain a length of woven wire fence 3 to 4 feet tall and long enough to make an enclosure about 6 to 8 feet in diameter. If you have very few leaves, make the circle only a few feet across. Secure it into a "corral" ring, and stake it to stand up stiffly on its own.

2. When the leaves start to fall, rake them up and throw them into the corral. When the first layer is about a foot deep, wet it down. Then turn on some lively Mediterranean folk music, don your workboots, and hop inside. Stomp the leaves down into a tight layer.

3. Then shovel a thin covering of soil over the leaf layer and scatter a handful of general-purpose granular fertilizer evenly on top. If you have chickens or livestock, their manure is perfect for this.

4. The next time you rake leaves, put another foot-deep layer in the corral, turn on the music, and have another go at it. Repeat the process until the enclosure is as full as you can get it. In warmer climates, it might be ready by late spring, but in colder climates you may have to wait until the end of summer.

CHEAP-SCAPES CHOICES: Here's a good alternative to a chipper/shredder machine for tightwad gardeners who own a rotary lawn mower with a catcher bag. Rake up your leaves and spread them into a layer or flat-topped pile about 2 to 3 inches thick. With the catcher bag attached, slowly "mow" the pile, and you'll discover that the leaves are sucked up into the blade, chopped to a medium texture, and neatly deposited in your catcher bag. All you have to do is empty the bag into a compost pile or leaf-mold bin or directly into the garden as a soil amendment or mulch. Recently new lawn mowers have been designed with special features to do this, but they are terribly expensive and require a lot more maintenance.

GETTING DIRT

Some landscaping projects require new soil to create mounds, fill raised beds, repair washouts and erosion, or level out sloping ground. But not all dirt is the same. "Topsoil" is a loose term and does not really define what you're getting in a load. Silty loam deposits along riverbanks and flood plains are typically light, sandy, and medium-textured. They also tend to be chock full of aggressive weed seeds. Rich, dark agricultural soils can be highly fertile but are mostly clay, which tends to pack into clods when wet.

The cheapest way to obtain soil is to find a source yourself and haul it in a pickup truck or trailer, but this is a big undertaking and probably not a good idea for beginner gardeners. Those who have not yet developed a keen eye for quality soil may end up with a solid mass of hardpan dense as concrete that looked so soft and crumbly when first excavated.

For projects where drainage is important, such as vegetable gardens, or when filling raised masonry planters, it's a good idea to ask for a sample of the soil or visit the "borrow" site to take a look. Another trick is to get the first load of an excavation job, which usually contains all the topsoil. It's always better to err on the side of rapid drainage than to risk your garden health on heavy, unworkable clay.

Even if you do find an ideal soil source, you must obtain permission to take it from the site. Second, you have to fill your truck with shovels by hand, then haul it home and unload it. If the vehicle is borrowed, you'll have to return that too *after* you've thoroughly cleaned out the bed. Sounds complicated? You bet. Good dirt is hard to come by.

FOR INTERMEDIATE AND ADVANCED GARDENERS ONLY

It's best for beginners to buy their soil from a reputable landscape-supply company to avoid problems. More advanced gardeners should not underestimate how much dirt it will take to raise the elevation of a square foot of ground just one inch. Soils tend to fluff up when disturbed, and once spread out will compact into a layer that's much thinner than expected. In most cases a job of any size demands that you pay a trucking company to obtain and transport the soil for you. Buying the dirt itself is not particularly expensive, except in regions such as the desert South-

IMPORTANT VOLUME EQUIVALENTS

In order to know how much soil or surfacing material you'll need, figure the quantities in cubic measure. Most bulk materials sold by the truckload are costed out by the cubic yard. If you buy bagged materials, each container will be labeled with the number of cubic feet it contains.

1 cubic foot = 1,728 cubic inches

1 cubic yard = 27 cubic feet

1 cubic foot of material should cover an area roughly 1,728 square inches or 144 square feet (12 feet by 12 feet) in size at a depth of 1 inch.

west, where soils are naturally infertile and obtaining quality topsoil is costly. The real expense is in transporting soil from the source to your home. The more distant the source, the higher your trucking cost. There's also more than just the truck to consider.

For example, to obtain soil from point A and move it to point B requires a dump truck. To load the truck, which averages 6 to 12 cubic yards per load, you'll need heavy equipment, such as a backhoe or loader. It would take all day for two or three men to fill a truck with shovels, so the loader and the loader operator are indispensable. Once the dump truck is full it must travel to your home. If you live in an urban area, there may be restrictions as to which roadways a truck of that size and weight can legally pass over, which can lengthen the period or distance of travel and thus increase prices. You may find that local trucking companies charge a flat fee, which will be the same whether you are buying manure, gravel, or sand. That's because it is the transportation, not the cost of the material, which dictates how much you pay for the load.

The best way to track down sources of topsoil is through local trucking companies, because they are the ones who are transporting quantities for the construction industry. Consult the Yellow Pages and call around to find out which ones serve your area and whether they have access to soil or other bulk materials. In my county, a 10-to-12-cubic-yard dump truck load of gravel or topsoil costs $150 per load, but prices may be far higher in urban areas.

One of the best sources of free soil is swimming pool excavations. To dig this massive hole, contractors usually have a backhoe on site, which is also used to load the spoils into a nearby dumptruck, which must haul it away. If you inform them ahead of time that you want the dirt, they are likely to drive straight to your house and dump the load free of charge. This saves them gas and allows the truck to be freed up much sooner. The only disadvantage is that the load may contain topsoil along with less desirable cement-like soil types from deeper down, such as adobe, hardpan, or caliche.

Other contractors who deal in dirt are listed in the Yellow Pages under these headings: blasting, concrete, demolition, engineering, excavation, foundation, grading, masonry, trenching, landscape, pipeline, road building, sewer, and well drilling.

SAND

Sand is a valuable component for lightening heavy clays or for creating porous, well-drained potting soil. Not all sand is the same. Aggregate sand—sand and gravel used in the mixing of concrete, mortar, and plaster—is readily available because of the widespread demand for it in construction. You will find it moderately priced with the addition of trucking charges. It is broken and sharp to better bind concrete. River sand—sand that originates directly from a waterway, is rounded, has been worn smooth, and packs down tightly. Wherever there are rivers you'll find river sand. Many cactus-soil mixes specifically designate sharp sand, because river sand settles in too densely for these sensitive roots.

Sometimes there are ancient dry riverbeds far from any water course that are rich in aggregates. Gravel companies and even private landowners mine these riverbeds and dry deposits of sand and gravel. Gravel companies are not always interested in sand and may charge you a pittance for a pickup load. Often there's a loader on site, and for a few bucks your truck can be quickly filled, eliminating the need to shovel it manually. In fact, gravel companies may have no interest in pockets of rich silt, which also makes fine garden soil. Sand and gravel have dozens of uses in gardening—from soil improvers to surfacing for walkways and even sports courts. Go to the source, aggregate companies (under this heading in the Yellow Pages), to save big.

TIGHTWAD GARDENING TIP: Beware of harvesting sand from coastal beaches. Sand, rock, shells, and seaweed all contain very high concentrations of salt. Beach sand added to any garden guarantees future problems, as salt is toxic to most plants and particularly dangerous around acid-loving plants. Stones, shells, and seaweed used for decorative purposes in rock gardens are equally undesirable, as the salt may leach out of them gradually and poison the surrounding soil. Thoroughly wash these marine objets d'art with detergent before putting them in the garden.

CHAPTER 3

SAVING WATER

Drought Strategies and Lower Bills

 The population of the United States is growing at a steady rate. This means that no matter how much water is available today, it may be insufficient to meet the needs of future generations. It is the responsibility of every gardener to use water carefully and avoid waste.

In order to save water and lower bills, budget gardeners should always be aware of just how much of this precious stuff is being used or wasted in the garden. In fact, there is an important relationship between how we water and just how drought-tolerant a plant will ultimately be. Just as we have developed a new approach to recyclable household materials, so should we heighten our awareness of all water uses, both indoors and out, by applying the guidelines set forth in this chapter.

EARTH AND WATER

It's essential for the gardener to understand how water behaves in and around soils to know the most efficient way of getting it to the roots of thirsty plants.

Percolation rate is the speed at which water is absorbed by soil. Water percolates quickest through sandy soil, but is very slow to saturate clays.

41

Surface evaporation denotes water that evaporates out of soil unprotected from direct sun and wind, particularly in dry climates.

Root zone is the area of soil reached by the plant's roots.

Deep rooting denotes plants that are naturally more able to survive drought than surface-rooted plants.

The best way to encourage a deeper root system is to water slowly, but to a great depth. With deep watering, plants root downward and may eventually encounter strata of permanently moist soil. The time between deep waterings is much longer than with other types of irrigation, so you need not water as often. Under the infrequent regimen of deep watering you are assured the greatest degree of drought tolerance in the plants you grow.

DROUGHT-TOLERANT PLANTS

Most drought-tolerant plants originate in climates that experience a long dry season. These species have evolved to cope with such conditions by growing quickly during the brief rains, their roots extending as deeply as possible to tap every bit of moisture hidden deep in the soil.

In nature, a drought-resistant plant species will begin deep rooting immediately after sprouting. The gardener's problem is that most landscape plants are container-grown, which confines the roots to the shape of the pot. After you plant them in the garden, it can take up to two years before the roots develop enough for the plant to take on some degree of drought tolerance. The way you water and the depth to which the soil is saturated during those first two years contribute to the size and effectiveness of the root system later on.

If you are concerned about water availability in the future, your long-term goal should be to replace thirsty plants with more drought-tolerant species. This assures you an attractive landscape even when water rationing is imposed. A total replacement of the landscape is expensive and requires a new watering system designed specifically for the needs of drought-tolerant plants.

If your problem is the cost of buying water that is in good supply, you must weigh the price of new planting against your expenses. For example, if you want to save $100 per year on the water bill, and it costs $500 to replant your garden, then it will take five years to recoup your investment and break even. It pays off to sit down and compare your costs to see whether new plants will indeed save you money in the long run.

LOW-PRESSURE IRRIGATION

When water is in short supply, traditional spray systems become very inefficient. This is partly because fine mists of water are vulnerable to evaporation as they fly through the air and can also be blown off course by wind. Drip systems avoid this loss by delivering water directly to the base of each plant. Flow rates are so low each drop soaks directly into the soil, the moisture is not subject to surface evaporation, and the saturation encourages adventurous rooting. You can install a drip

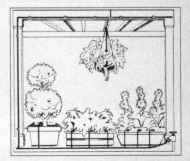

DRIP-SYSTEM LAYOUTS

There are dozens of ways to adapt a low-pressure drip system to fit your yard. Because the lines are flexible and simple to assemble without special tools, virtually anyone can do it. LEFT: *Plants located in rows are the easiest to water with a drip system. The key is to allow at least one emitter per plant, although you can use more if you wish.* CENTER: *Larger trees need far more water than is supplied by just one emitter. Here a single line is placed away from the trunk but still within the outer edges of the canopy. It is arranged in a circular shape, with emitters located at equal distances from one another to provide even water distribution.* RIGHT: *One of the first applications for drip systems was for watering plants in pots. It's messy and difficult to soak potted patio plants, because they drain out all over the ground. This is also the case with hanging plants, particularly moss baskets, and many gardeners have been drenched trying to get potting soil in suspended containers evenly wet. Running a single $1/4$-inch drip-system line into the pot is so easy, and plants are healthier in the long run because of more consistent soil-moisture levels.*

Raindrip Inc.

system in an existing landscape, although drip emitters are not suited to large areas of lawn or ground cover. Each plant will require one or more emitters, so some creativity on your part may be necessary to ensure that everything is adequately watered.

If a spray system is present, it's easy to adapt it to a drip system. Since drip systems function at low pressures, fittings don't have to be securely glued together. The simplest way to adapt a drip is to replace the spray head with a drip-system manifold cap. This is a screw-on fitting that is studded with nipples that fit easily into the plastic drip-system tubing. The final product can somewhat resemble an octopus. Be sure to install emitters, as indicated by the manufacturer's manual, because these are essential for pressure control.

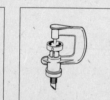

SOME COMPONENTS OF
A LOW-PRESSURE SYSTEM
There are many different parts and fittings that make up a functioning low-pressure system. TOP LEFT: *The "Y" filter is located close to the water source and traps any sediment that could clog the small orifices at each emitter.* TOP RIGHT: *Even if there is no current sprinkler system in place, you can install a drip system right off an outdoor hose bib.* BOTTOM LEFT: *You can enjoy the convenience of an automatic controller for your system even if it is attached to a hose bib. This clock will turn the system on and off at a preset time of day. Some of these controllers are solar-powered, others function on a battery. In either case there is no need to run electrical wires to take advantage of this feature of low-pressure systems. You can also use a timer that acts like a kitchen timer. You simply set the timer for the period of time you want the system to run, and the timer will automatically shut off the valve when time is up. This is also a handy feature for all your garden hoses, so the water is never left running.* BOTTOM RIGHT: *This detail shows the emitter of a micro-spray system. It sits on a small stake and is attached to ¼-inch lateral tubing.* Randrip Inc.

If no sprinklers are in place, or if you wish to abandon the old system, it's simple to set up drip irrigation lines from a nearby hose bib. Because drip systems are low-flow, you can water many more plants from a single line than you can with a spray system, which is limited by higher flow rates.

There is a new hybrid system called micro-spray, which combines the visibility of a spray system with the low-flow efficiency of a drip system. It is simple to install, but there is some evaporation loss, since it does spray. These heads don't water quite as deeply as a true drip system, but they provide a small-scale alternative for watering groundcovers and very low-growing spreading plants.

CHEAP-SCAPES CHOICES: You can go out and buy a book about drip or micro-spray irrigation systems, but there's a free way to gather this information too. Most home-improvement stores have special displays for drip irrigation systems and fittings made by a certain manufacturer. There you'll find free booklets and price lists published by the supplier that explain how drip systems work. Take one home and use it for reference, because most fittings are universal no matter who the manufacturer. Some booklets are very complete and cover planning, watering certain types of plants, and converting existing spray systems to drip, and provide tons of other useful tips and guidelines from experts. In addition, you can be sure this is up-to-date technology and the fittings illustrated will be readily available.

WATER-WISE WATERING

Amid the conveniences of modern-day living, we have developed a casual attitude about water use. If you had been born a hundred years ago and had to draw water from a well one bucket at a time, your awareness would be quite different. In fact, the ancient gardens of desert regions grew most plants in pots, where indoor waste water could be readily poured onto them. Just as we become aware of reusable or recyclable household products, so can we wake up to our wasteful patterns of water use.

If you are watering with a traditional spray system, cut the flow rate *but not coverage* by replacing the current heads with those that deliver water at a slower rate. Choose low-flow heads that spray the exact pattern and radius as the old ones. A standard spray head may deliver 1.5 gallons per minute, whereas a low-flow head with the same coverage delivers just 0.75 gallon per minute. This difference can cut your water bills and work better for soils with slow percolation rates by reducing

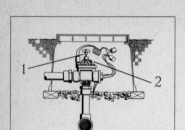

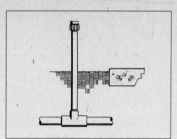

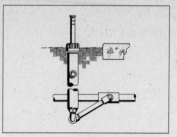

ELECTRIC SOLENOID VALVE
An automatically controlled sprinkler valve can be located aboveground or in a valve box, as this one is. There are two manual controls on this valve. The flow control is #1. It can be adjusted to allow more or less water to flow through the system. Don't adjust this, because if it is turned too low, it may leave sprinkler heads at the end of the line without sufficient flow to operate properly. Though smaller, #2 is the "bleeder valve," which can be used to open the valve without using the automatic controller. This one comes in handy when you're fine-tuning or repairing the system.

FIXED-RISER SPRINKLER
This is how most sprinkler heads appear underground. The feeder line is constructed with a "T" fitting that supports the riser. Risers screw into the "T," whereas the other two connections to the feeder line are permanently glued. If a fixed riser is run over, hit, or crushed aboveground, the impact may have cracked the underground "T." If there is any sign of water, excavate the entire "T," then turn on the valve to see if there is any leakage. Hairline cracks can be difficult to find, but they can waste a lot of water if you don't find them.

POP-UP HEAD ON SWING JOINT
This detail shows how a pop-up head functions and at what level it is set in the soil. Since these heads can be expensive, a swing joint provides some flexibility so you don't have to use as many heads, but it can be more difficult to repair.

runoff. Compared with a drip system, emitters deliver water so slowly it is gauged in gallons per *hour*.

AVOID THESE COMMON WATER-WASTING MISTAKES:

1. Forgotten garden hoses left running or not turned completely off will trickle unnoticed until someone uses the hose again. Purchase an automatic timer for each hose bib; it automatically turns off if you forget it.

2. Water can leak from broken water lines, sprinkler lines, or risers.

3. Leaking garden hoses, couplers, and hose bibs waste a lot of water. Leaks occur when rubber parts inside have deteriorated. Keep new rubber garden-hose

washers on hand. Replace any leaky hose bibs (outdoor faucets) that drip when turned off.

4. Poorly adjusted sprinkler heads throw water on unplanted surfaces. Heads blocked by plants or tall lawn grass aren't efficient.

5. Watering on a schedule, even when the soil is still moist. It is common for people to forget to readjust or turn off automatic sprinklers in wet weather.

6. Failure to adjust watering frequency as seasons change. This can result in too much or not enough water.

7. Watering during the heat of the day or in windy weather, when evaporation rates are highest.

Irrigation Maintenance Tasks

1. If the watering system is operated by an automatic timer, inspect the control panel at least once a month. Run the clock through all its stations, and while watering, go out and inspect the system. Make adjustments to duration of watering times to eliminate any unnecessary runoff. Turn the system off in wet weather, but be sure to leave a note indoors to remind you to turn it back on again when things dry out.

2. If the system is manual, open each valve and inspect the heads. Be aware of how much time passes before runoff results. Make a note of that time for each valve in case you forget.

3. Some potential problems that need immediate repair show up only while lines are pressurized. While testing each valve either manually or with the automatic controller, look for these problems:

- Broken heads, which result in dry spots. Replace heads as needed.
- Heads that are out of adjustment, which result in overly dry or overly wet spots. Readjust head to original throw pattern.
- Risers that are not tall enough to spray over plants or turf that has grown up in front of the head, resulting in limited coverage and dry spots. For shrub-planter areas, simply replace the current riser with one that is tall enough to spray over

the plants. If pop-up sprinklers are in use, replace current head with one that pops up higher.

- Pop-up heads that are jammed and not extending as they should. Remove head, inspect for any damage, then clean out the inside. Grains of sand can become lodged between the housing and the central portion that pops up where water pressure is insufficient to dislodge them.
- Gear-driven heads can be jammed and not turning properly. Remove head and thoroughly clean and oil the gears inside.
- Signs of water on the soil surface, silt, and other indications of broken lines. Excavate the pipe for a thorough inspection. If fittings or pipe is cracked or broken, replace as needed.
- Silt buildup around heads, indicating a broken riser. Excavate soil to the depth of the lateral line to inspect the "T" fitting and the riser that supports the head. If any are damaged, replace as needed.

4. If you are watering with a drip system, regular inspection is important. Turn on each valve and do the following:

- Inspect each emitter to be sure it has not clogged up or become restricted. Remove and clean clogged emitters. Emitters are inexpensive, and it's worthwhile to replace any that are marginal, damaged, or not functioning properly.
- Follow each supply line from the valve to the last head and inspect for signs of moisture. This low-pressure system doesn't exhibit cracks as readily as high-pressure spray systems do. Slow leaks from hairline cracks can waste water. Repair or replace as necessary.
- There is a flush plug or end clamp at the far end of each line. To flush any accumulated debris, sediment, algae, or mineral buildup out of the feeder lines, simply remove the plug, open the valve, allow water to flow freely for a few seconds, then replace the end plug.

5. If you are using a micro-spray system, turn on each valve and inspect every head. Plants may have grown up in front of them to block coverage. Add new heads or relocate existing ones to restore even coverage to all plants.

TIPS FOR MORE EFFICIENT WATER USE

1. Water early in the morning when municipal water pressure is consistent and your system will function at peak efficiency.
2. Do not water in windy weather or during the heat of the day.
3. Check soil moisture before you water, and water only when it is dry.
4. Mulch all planters to reduce surface evaporation.
5. Use a garden hose set at very slow drip to deep-water trees and shrubs.
6. Keep weeds that compete with landscape plants for water under control.
7. Mow the lawn higher to keep soil shaded and reduce surface evaporation.
8. Water the lawn for half the time it needs, then wait an hour before watering for the remaining time alloted to reduce runoff and deepen soil moisture.

6. If you are using any type of low-pressure system, clean out the filter frequently. It is located close to the valve or hose bib that supplies the water. Where water mineral content is high, the filter can fill up quickly and limit flow. This is an important factor in plant health and the efficiency of the system.

When you make PVC (plastic) pipe repairs with a hacksaw and glue, be sure to keep the lines free of any debris. Soil particles and shavings from your saw can enter lines and be forced up into the sprinkler head. Just before you glue in the last fitting, remove the last head on the line, then open the valve and flush the system. This pushes any accumulations out of the system.

WATER HARVESTING AND UNORTHODOX REUSE OF HOUSEHOLD WATER

Long before sprinkler systems and pressurized water, farm wives were forced to water their flowers with well water, but if that was in short supply, they resorted to rain barrels. These would catch the water draining from the roof and hold it for future use. In very dry climates, people have begun to resurrect this old idea using cheap 50-gallon drums attached to downspouts in rain gutters. Later in the year, water can be siphoned out of the barrel or drawn by the bucketful for emergency water when drought hits. This is one of the few options available to help your trees and shrubs survive water rationing.

There is a lot of discussion about gray water these days, because in many cities and counties it is strictly forbidden. What is gray water? It is simply the used water that drains into a septic system or the public sewer. But there are different types of gray water, and some are more suitable as alternative water sources for landscapes than others.

One reason for the gray-water laws was public health. Water from the kitchen sink and toilets can be tainted with dangerous bacteria, and is not healthful or suitable for any purpose. But water that drains from the shower, bath, and laundry can be valuable and fairly clean. The biggest cause of poor water quality from these sources is soaps that contain strong perfumes, bleach, fabric softeners, and other chemical additives. If this water is used in landscaping, these chemicals can build up to toxic levels around plants, but they will eventually be diluted by the rain. Using chemical-free laundry detergent and mild organic shampoo or soap can render such gray water a viable alternative source of water. In fact, some of the nitrates and phosphates in detergents add nutrients that can make plants healthier if they are not concentrated in too great a quantity. Laundry gray water is the easiest to harvest: remove the black drain line from the standpipe to the sewer, then route it through a hole in the floor, under the house, and out through the foundation vent. For slab foundation, it should be routed through a wall. Check with a plumber before proceeding, to avoid missteps.

CHAPTER 4

SHOPPING PLANTS

How to Buy and Where

One of the most satisfying things about gardening is obtaining new plants and adding them to the garden. Plant sellers range from huge garden centers to garage sales, and the prices vary accordingly. But quality is important too, because plants are living things that should be in good health if they are to survive transplanting and grow vigorously. Smart shoppers weigh price against the quality of the plant to find the best deals.

A lot depends on your budget and horticultural knowledge and the amount of time you have to devote to gardening. There are some excellent bargains on discounted or sometimes free plants that are ailing, and under a practiced hand these can be nursed back to health. But this situation can spell "wasted cash" for a novice gardener who may not have the knowledge to give such a plant new life.

It's a good idea to view shopping for plants as you would shopping for groceries. Everyone knows that going to the market without a list can end up costing you a lot more than if you came prepared and purchased only those items you needed. The same applies when going to the nursery, because of the strong temptation to purchase anything in bloom. Unless you have money to burn, never go plant shopping without some idea of what you want. If a plant really catches your eye, write down the name, then go home and read all about it to see if there's a place for it in the garden and if you can care for it.

WHAT TO BUY

It is easy to view a landscape plant as purely aesthetic, but its value is increased if we view it more as a crop. This is the way early hunter-gatherers saw wild plants that provided food and raw materials essential to life. We should expand our thinking of garden plants and seek those that fulfill a dual role. For example, the bay laurel, *Laurus nobilis*, is an attractive evergreen landscape tree that also provides an unlimited source of bay leaves for cooking. This makes it more valuable than a similar tree that is priced exactly the same but does not bear a usable crop. When choosing trees, or other types of plants, always consider this secondary value. Some of the most interesting secondary uses for plants include decorations, flowers, aromatic foliage, fall color, fruits, nuts, or seed pods.

Trees offer some of the best secondary crops. A dwarf apple tree not only adds spring flowers to your landscape, it also produces an annual crop of fruit. Fortunately, dwarf or semidwarf sizes are smaller overall and fit well into an ornamental landscape. If you live in a warm climate, a citrus tree is a better bargain in evergreens than a privet, because of its scented flowers and brightly colored fruit. Likewise, a rose that produces plentiful, large hips is more valuable than one that just offers pretty flowers.

THE FOLLOWING LISTS INCLUDE EXAMPLES OF PLANTS THAT PROVIDE VARIOUS TYPES OF SECONDARY CROPS:

Edible Fruit: apple, plum, cherry, pear, peach, apricot, citrus, fig, persimmon, blueberry, huckleberry, raspberry, blackberry, grapevine, kiwi.

Nuts: almond, chestnut, hickory, oak, pecan, walnut.

Berries for beauty, crafts, and wildlife: California pepper, crabapple, hawthorne, holly, serviceberry, cotoneaster, bush honeysuckle, viburnums, barberry.

Plants for colorful fall foliage: ash, Chinese tallow tree, dogwood, maidenhair tree, maple, oak, pistachio, redbud, sweet gum, barberry, burning bush.

Aromatic foliage: camphor, eucalyptus, bay laurel, conifers, California pepper, myrtle yarrow, santolina, lavender, sages, rosemary.

Cones or pods: carob, cedar, cypress, fir, hemlock, pine, mimosa, redbud, redwood, sequoia, spruce, sweet gum, locust.

LIVING CHRISTMAS TREES AND HOW TO RECYCLE DEAD ONES

Imagine how much you've spent over the years on Christmas trees that just get thrown away in January. Since today's trees are grown on farms, using an indoor tree is no threat to our forests, but you must purchase this disposable product each winter. In large cities like New York or Los Angeles, the cost is higher, and the tree may be very difficult to get home, especially if you don't own a vehicle suitable for the job. In addition, tens of millions of used holiday trees must be disposed of each year—a nightmare for landfill managers. It's always sad to see a dead, rejected plant lying out by the curb with a few strands of tinsel clinging to the brown needles hinting at its former glory.

Budget gardeners never throw away a cut tree after Christmas. If the tree has an X-shaped base nailed to the trunk it will stand up on its own. Store the tree upright in your veggie garden, and in spring bring it out as a snow pea trellis. Peas use thin tendrils to climb and require a delicate trellis that is thin enough. Stabilize the dead tree with weights on the base, then plant your peas around the outside.

Take advantage of the raw materials a Christmas tree produces. First, cut off all the side branches and use them for winter protection of garden plants, or strip off the dead needles and add them to the compost pile. The bare trunk can be sawn up into fireplace logs. It can also be left whole and stored on a flat surface to dry. During the summer use it to create a rustic arbor or to prop up loaded fruit tree branches.

Fortunately, you can eliminate the annual expense of buying a tree, the struggle to get it home, and the problems of disposal by starting a living Christmas-tree tradition. Living trees, once purchased and planted in the landscape, become a beautiful part of the garden. The first Christmas it will still be in its container and can be used indoors, but come spring it should be planted in the garden.

When designing landscapes for my clients, I always ask if they would like a pine, fir, or spruce in the front yard to decorate for the holidays. Although an indoor tree is the traditional way to celebrate the holidays, an outdoor tree decorated with weatherproof lights and ornaments can be just as satisfying. Decorations made to feed winter birds add even more charm. Plant them in full view of the front window for best enjoyment from indoors. If you live in a cold winter climate, real snow on an outdoor tree is always more beautiful than artificial flocking.

Before you choose a living Christmas tree, be sure it is a species that grows well in your climate. Many of the most beautiful and symmetrical conifers cannot thrive in very warm winters and may gradually decline no matter how much special care you provide. If in doubt, discuss it with a local garden-center expert, because they will carry living Christmas species appropriate for your area. Also keep in mind that many trees, such as Scotch pine, are gradually sheared into more conical shapes. These, as with all topiary, may require shearing once or twice a year for best effect, but you're then assured a perfectly symmetrical tree for the holidays. Thanks to electric hedge clippers, shearing a large outdoor Christmas tree is easier than ever.

HERE ARE A FEW SPECIES POPULAR AS OUTDOOR CHRISTMAS TREES:

Alpine fir—*Abies lasiocarpa*

Balsam fir—*Abies balsamea*

Colorado blue spruce—*Picea pungens "Glauca"*

Douglas fir—*Pseudotsuga menziesii*

Eastern red cedar—*Juniperus virginiana*

Grand fir—*Abies grandis*

Norway spruce—*Picea excelsa*

Norway spruce—*Picea abies*

Red pine—*Pinus resinosa*

Scotch pine—*Pinus sylvestris*

Southern balsam fir—*Abies Fraseri*

White spruce—*Picea glauca*

Salvaging Plants—Not Recommended for Beginners

In my early years I worked for one of California's most famous creative retail garden centers. There was a strict rule forbidding employees to salvage plants out of the company Dumpster, where some beautiful specimens ended up, along with chipped clay pots and distorted wire topiary forms. I couldn't stand seeing those beauties buried in the landfill, and my paycheck was too small to allow such decorative purchases. So on the sly I salvaged them for my own house and garden where I could appreciate them and nurture them back to health.

If you are the adventurous sort, take a peek into the garden-center Dumpster before you go inside to shop. If you are less nervy, simply ask the garden-center owner for any plants he or she plans to throw out. If you're lucky, they will cooperate and set aside anything with potential. But to keep this relationship going, be sure to pick up plants on the same day each week so they don't pile up. Most garden centers, particularly those in the city, simply don't have room to hold your plants, so it is essential that you pick up as frequently as the manager deems appropriate.

Another good source of salvage plants is landscape contractors. If a contractor is relandscaping a home or commercial building, there are bound to be a good number of plants to be torn out. Most end up in the dump, but plants such as cacti and succulents will live for quite a while out of the ground and are always worth salvaging from a "demolition" zone. The same applies to palms, which hold much of their moisture in their trunks and will tolerate the most brutal treatment. Where bulbs were growing or naturalized, the grading, trenching, and other construction activities spell their demise unless some concerned salvage junkie gets in there and digs them out. Contractors simply can't afford to pay a laborer to poke around with a spading fork for all the bulbs hidden in the soil of their job site.

In your regular travels around town, keep an eye out for remodeling or demolition sites that may be removing plants during the process. You can also phone landscape contractors in your area and ask if they have any remodeling jobs coming up that might yield plants. Be sure to inquire if they have any unwanted beauties sitting around in the equipment yard—they often do. Sometimes the contractor can resell them to another customer, but often they die of neglect before an opportunity arises.

Plants worth salvaging are those that are tolerant of transplanting. Anything that does not like root disturbance is not worth the trouble.

GROUPS OF PLANTS THAT ARE IDEAL CANDIDATES FOR SALVAGE

Most herbaceous perennials	Shrubby willows
Cacti	Smaller palms
Succulents	Strap-leafed plants
Bulbs	Peonies
Ornamental grasses	Lilies
Roses	Yucca
Herbs	Ferns
Dwarf shrubs	Vines

HOW TO BUY A QUALITY PLANT

The surge in gardening interest has resulted in great changes in the places where plants are sold. It used to be that the local nursery supplied everyone, but now a wide array of retail outlets are carrying plants. Before going to the obvious retail sources, consider specialty sales, which may yield a greater diversity, the rare and unusual, very low prices, and a hassle-free environment. Keep your eye on the local gardening columns in the newspaper, and if you are lucky there will be a gardening-event calendar, which you should clip and place on the refrigerator so you won't miss an opportunity.

The gardening editors at newspapers are often the kingpins of what's happening in the local gardening universe. They know all about the groups, societies, and special events that only those who are horticulturally "in the know" keep up on. If you want to contact local chapters of these groups but don't know where to begin, give the editor a call, send a fax, or write a letter.

LOCAL NONRETAIL PLANT SALES

Each year, more and more charity groups are discovering the value of fund raising through plant sales. This has always been the territory of garden societies, but today other folks are getting in on the act to raise cash for schools and other nonprofit groups. Although sales not connected with horticultural groups may sell nothing more than vegetable and flower seedlings, they can still have some great deals.

For more sophisticated gardeners, keep abreast of activities of the following organizations to stock your garden with the rare and unusual at rock-bottom prices.

AMERICAN PLANT SOCIETIES

There is an official society for each of the following types of plants: begonia, boxwood, bromeliad, cactus, camellia, chrysanthemum, daffodil, dahlia, delphinium, fern, fuchsia, geranium, gesneriad, gladiola, gloxinia, gourd, hemerocallis, hibiscus, holly, hosta, iris, ivy, lilac, lily, magnolia, orchid, palm, penstemon, peony, primrose, rhododendron, rose, and succulent.

Whenever these societies want to raise money to support their activities, they often hold a plant sale and show. If you join the societies, you'll get to know the aficionados who grow a single type of plant in enormous quantities. Often these folks are deluged with the more common vigorous varieties and must weed them out to make room for the precious, rare additions to their collections. You get to pick up their overflow for pennies and benefit from newsletters and other membership goodies.

UNIVERSITIES AND COLLEGES

Many educational institutions hold plant sales at the end of each quarter or semester to raise money for the ornamental horticulture program. They sell everything from grafted fruit trees to greenhouse plants and vegetable seedlings. Schools with greenhouses and extensive ornamental horticulture or agriculture facilities are more likely to have sales.

BOTANICAL GARDENS AND ARBORETUMS

When the botanical garden must divide a perennial or dig its exotic bulbs, it usually has some left over. This type of material is sold to raise money for these plant museums. Desert gardens sell desert plants, rock gardens sell alpines, and glassed conservatories sell hothouse delights. If you become a supporting member or docent for these gardens, you'll get first crack at the sale plants before they are offered to the public.

LOCAL RETAIL STORES

Buying plants and gardening supplies is the art of balancing quality with price. There are now so many retail stores selling plants and related products that it gets overwhelming. Sometimes convenience overrides quality and price. Which choice is the best source for the products you seek is up to you and depends on your lifestyle.

GARDEN CENTER OR NURSERY

The industry has changed the name from nursery to garden center, which better describes the broad assortment of plants and products available. Items are more expensive here, but plant quality and choice are far better than anywhere else.

HOME-IMPROVEMENT STORE

The home-improvement store is one of the very best places to buy plants, and these businesses are putting a big dent in the sales of garden centers. They may carry a good number of trees and larger shrubs. The best selection is in spring, but supplies in warm climate states are more diverse year-round. Perhaps the best prices to be found here are on bedding plants, garden supplies, bagged manures, bagged ground bark, and tools, particularly at national chain stores, which buy in quantity.

DEPARTMENT STORE

Large-scale discount stores allow one-stop shopping for house and garden supplies. Many have outdoor garden shops with mostly annuals, perennials, showy vines, shrubs, and the occasional tree. There are also lots of supplies, pots, and potting soil.

SUPERMARKET

This is a convenient source, but selection is usually limited to seasonal bedding plants and house plants. Supplies include small quantities of potting soil and name-brand commercial fertilizers.

DRUGSTORE

Chain stores may have a generous garden-supply section with pest-control products, fertilizers, and small tools. Plants, typically annuals, may or may not be sold.

CAVEAT EMPTOR—INSPECT BEFORE YOU BUY

If you have to pay for a plant, it should be of the best quality. But in a typical display you'll find that some individuals are healthier than others, and unless you take the time to choose a good one, you may pay top dollar for an inferior product. Don't be in a hurry, and try to have a shopping list prepared before you go. Use this handy checklist of inspection pointers as a guide.

1. There are three aspects to a plant you should examine: (a) roots, (b) shape, (c) health.
2. Roots. Container stock: Avoid roots on the surface, roots coming out the drain holes, roots matted together. Balled and burlapped: Avoid dry, loose rootball. Bare root: Avoid dry, damaged, crushed, and broken roots. Avoid plants with too few roots.
3. Trunk. Avoid gouges, scars, tears from lost branches, nicks around the bottom. Trunks of trees and shrubs should be upright, straight, and evenly balanced, not slanted or twisted.
4. Branching. Avoid bare spots, broken branches, oversized branches that don't conform to shape, lopsided form. Shrubs lacking lower branches or those that are poorly shaped now will never repair themselves.
5. Foliage. Avoid discoloration, unusual leaf drop, wilted leaves, curled-up leaves.

6. Bedding plants. Avoid spindly stems, poor shape, irregular growth habits, under-sized buds or leaves.
7. Pest damage. Avoid plants with little white flies, unusual granular material coming out of pot holes, white fuzzy cotton balls in the branch joints, spots on undersides of leaves.

Never assume that, just because a plant is for sale locally, it is suited to your climate. Retail plant sellers often carry colorful exotic plants in warm months to catch your eye and increase sales. Don't believe everything you read is true either. Plants advertised as miracle problem solvers are usually common garden varieties promoted under less than honest terms.

All garden-plant salespeople are not expert gardeners. More plants have been sold on bad advice than on any other factor, and since plant sellers have one goal—to sell you plants—there can be a conflict of interest. Remember, if you buy a plant that is destined to fail in your climate, you might as well pour dollars down the toilet bowl. Find a reputable garden center with well-trained employees, or obtain advice from experts who have nothing to sell you but their love of horticulture.

Each and every plant has its own preference for sunlight. You must choose a plant to fit the exposure, not the other way around. Pay attention to conditions in the nursery. If the plant has been growing under a canopy of shade cloth, don't thrust it right out into the sun. It requires time for gradual adjustment. Never scrimp on quality when buying expensive trees and shrubs. Bedding plants are more variable, but unless you're the Florence Nightingale of the horticultural world, put your money on quality and you win every time.

You have a right to the very best plant in the display. It's okay to look at every one before making your final selection. After all, it will become a part of your garden and should be as beautiful as possible. A big, vigorous, well-formed plant is bound to grow better.

Most nurseries cannot carry all the plants that are available in the marketplace. Although a plant may not be currently in stock, it can usually be obtained by special order from a wholesale grower. A quality garden center should be eager to fill your special orders to keep you as a steady customer. If they are unwilling to order plants for you, go somewhere else.

THINGS TO REMEMBER

Landscape trees take decades to mature and represent a long-term investment. You should choose a tree very carefully. Many people fail to discover that they planted the wrong tree until a decade later, when problems arise. By that time the damage is done and you have no choice but to start over. First the bad tree must be removed by professionals, who are expensive to hire, then a new tree must be purchased and planted.

A shrub will serve various purposes in your landscape. Like trees, shrubs grow slowly and take time to mature. Some can develop into tree-sized proportions, so you must be sure you select the proper species for the space provided in your landscape. Shrubs can grow in their natural shape or be sheared into hedges or even topiary. Be sure your shrub is the right size for the space *at maturity*.

If you can't plant right away, store nursery plants in the shade and water them every day. Never buy a plant that is not labeled, because it may be an entirely different species that is far too large or too small for your garden. If a tree or shrub dies just after you plant it, call the garden center. They should replace the plant, because such quick death indicates there may have been a preexisting problem.

Gift plants such as azaleas and poinsettias purchased from florists probably won't grow if planted out in the garden. These are specialty plants that are pampered for this purpose and not prepared for open garden conditions.

Never leave the nursery stake on trees or vines attached after you plant them out, since they aren't nearly strong enough to support your tree. Instead, replace them with a stronger stake anchored in undisturbed soil in the bottom of your planting hole.

CHAPTER 5

PLANT-PROPAGATION PAYOFFS

"Propagation" is a common horticultural term for creating new plants. But what makes it more important to budget gardeners is that it means they can acquire new plants *free*. Once you discover how simple plant propagation can be, you'll be able to enlarge your garden without spending a penny. Chances are the way you look at gardening will be changed as well. Suddenly you'll see plants everywhere in a new light, recognizing those that are suitable parent material and figuring out ways to obtain a slip or seed.

SEX IN THE GARDEN

Before you begin, a brief introduction to sex in the garden is in order. Each plant contains a certain gene pool of traits, just as we do. During pollination, a whole new set of genes is introduced from a second plant of the same species, just as with human reproduction. The two sets of genes combine to create seeds that are totally unique, none carrying exactly the same genetic material as either parent. As a result, if you plant the seed, chances are it will be different from the parent in some way.

A new plant grown directly from the tissue of another will contain exactly the same genetic material as its parent, like an identical twin. This method is called vegetative, or asexual, propagation. For example, a new potato plant is always grown from pieces of potato tuber from a mother plant, and never by seed, ensuring they are all identical. The same applies to a cutting that is rooted and then planted. The three simplest methods of asexual, or vegetative, propagation include rooted cuttings, layering, and division.

The method you ultimately choose to reproduce a plant will be based on the species of the original. Some plants simply defy propagation no matter what method you use, or they take such a long time they aren't worth the effort. Plants such as eucalyptus must be grown from seed, because they refuse to root from cuttings. The most rewarding plants for propagation are like the geranium, rugged and eager to root. Some beginner gardeners have difficulty propagating plants only because they don't research the methods best suited for each plant.

GROWING PLANTS FROM SEED

Plants that are most often grown from seed are annuals such as bedding plants, cutting flowers, or vegetables. Annuals are quick to sprout, because they must mature, flower, and set seed in a single season. This eagerness to sprout and a high rate of genetic uniformity are what makes them so well suited to growing from seed. Some perennials are nearly as eager to germinate, but as a rule they are more often propagated vegetatively.

You can collect your seeds directly from plants or buy them. We don't often allow our plants to go to seed in landscapes, because this stops the flowering process and may spell the demise of the plant well before the end of the season. But should the seed be available, wait until the seed pod has fully matured and is beginning to open on its own before releasing the seed. Collect your seed or the entire pod, sift out debris such as flower petals, and store it in a cool, dry place for next year. Look for seed pods in your own garden, along the wayside, or in friends' yards where plants have been allowed to finish their annual cycle.

Last year I collected the seed from my largest gourd to use in this year's garden. The vines died back prematurely, and although the gourd and its seed appeared perfect, I found out the hard way that the seed had not developed properly. This year I planted the home-gathered seed and other seed purchased from a supply house. The vines that resulted from my own seed were spindly and "poor doers," with pitiful, tiny gourds. Those from store-bought seed were enormous and nearly took over the entire garden. This illustrates how unreliable home-gathered seed can be, and not only were all my efforts in soil preparation and nurturing these reluctant plants wasted, but my gourd harvest was greatly reduced.

Buying seed allows you to grow new and different plants that may be otherwise unavailable to you. Seed collecting can be tedious, and if your time is limited, it's best to purchase quality seed that is sure to germinate. It is discouraging to spend time tending a seed bed only to discover a few weeks later that the seed is not viable. This can happen if you use old seed or if seed you collected did not mature properly.

TIGHTWAD GARDENING TIP: Never scrimp on seed. The seed of some plants loses its viability over just a few seasons, with the germination rates dwindling each year. Many gardeners have unhappily discovered this fact and as a result insist on new seed each season, because the cost of a few packets is far less expensive than the time required to replant what did not grow. Discounted seed at retail stores carried over from the previous season is not a good buy no matter how cheap the price.

It's a good idea to keep your stored seed well organized. Anyone who grows a large vegetable garden knows how many of the little packets can accumulate in your seed drawer. In the process of sorting through them, seed is spilled, the packages tear, and viability is reduced by such handling. Mice are also a big problem and will decimate an entire seed supply in just a few nights.

The answer: Buy a portable office box, one of those plastic file boxes with lids and a handle where documents are stored. The beauty of these is they are made of molded plastic and the whole thing can be carried out to the garden and set down in the wet without any damage to the contents. Not only that, but the plastic lids are tight fitting and rodent-proof and help keep your seed viable much longer than other types of containers. Label your files with seed types and perhaps the year they were purchased as well.

Those little plastic film canisters also make perfect seed containers because they are so well made and have tight-fitting lids. The tops of some are of a rough texture so you can write the seed type and the date on top. These are really helpful when storing seed such as that of poppies, which retains its viability far longer if refrigerated. The canisters don't take up much space, nor do they spill or disintegrate after long-term exposure to refrigeration moisture. You can also find snap-on salt-shaker lids for the canisters at stores that sell camping equipment. These handy lids are simply snapped into place, and then smaller seed can be shaken out without spilling.

SOWING SEED

Sowing seed is simple if you follow a few important guidelines. Virtually any well-drained container can be used as a seed bed as long as it holds together until it's time to transplant the seedlings to larger pots. See Chapter 7 for suggestions on household disposables you can recycle into seedling containers.

Some retail nurseries buy their perennial seedlings in little 2-inch pots, nurture them along, then transplant them to the more expensive 1-gallon pots. Often the nurseries have lots of these little pots and empty flats left over. If you ask, they may be glad to give you some they have on hand or will save them for you after their next shipment. Another good source of containers is landscape contractors. They frequently have left-over flats from groundcover plantings as well as handy 4-inch pots and even larger containers. The key is to catch them just after they plant a landscape, or make friends so you can call periodically to find out what's on their schedule.

CHEAP-SCAPES CHOICES: Because it takes only a short time to grow annuals from seed, it's okay to use tin cans. By the time they begin to rust the seedlings are ready to be planted out in the garden. Most restaurant kitchens throw out a virtual treasure trove of containers every day!

> Foods are packed in huge cans sometimes 6 or more inches in diameter, often larger than a 5-pound coffee can. The real prizes are tuna cans, which are large in diameter but not very deep. Restaurant-size frying oils are sold in huge plastic jugs—like those for liquid laundry detergent but even larger. The bottoms can be cut off to make first-class mini-flats that never rust or disintegrate. A standing recycling relationship with your local restaurants, delis, sandwich shops, hamburger stands, school cafeteria, and other food-service entities in your neighborhood not only helps the environment but assures you of an unending source of free pots.

It's a lot easier to start your seedlings in flats that hold dozens in one large container. Since these are purely functional, they need not be attractive or decorative, so virtually anything works. Here are some cheap or free alternatives using old or worn-out items:

Wooden dresser drawers (not Pressboard)	Cells of concrete blocks	Cat box
Discarded pots and pans	Fruit crates	
Automobile rims	Rusty wok	

Keep an eye out for sources of food-service containers that have clear-plastic dome lids so you can see the contents. Some have a tin-foil bottom and a clear top; others have a clear top and bottom connected on one side by a hinge. These function like miniature greenhouses, keeping the moisture in with a lid while allowing maximum sunlight through. All make first-class containers for sprouting seeds on the windowsill.

Seeds germinate best in lightweight, airy, finely textured rooting soil. It gets expensive to buy special bagged soils designated for seed beds, but these assure you a perfectly blended medium free of weed seeds. They are also sufficiently sterile to prevent damping off, a disease that rapidly kills seedlings in the overly moist, enclosed conditions that are ideal for seed germination. You can reduce the chances of damping off in your own potting soil by cooking it in an oven, but this is really inconvenient. Instead, be sure the soil is allowed to dry out occasionally during the germination process.

The classic recipe for homemade seed-bed soil:

1 part topsoil (introduces important microorganisms; avoid clay)

1 part sand (ensures that the mix is well drained)

1 part compost or leaf mold (provides organic matter that absorbs moisture)

If you have a compost pile, you can sometimes plant young plants and cuttings in the finished product as well, but if it's not thoroughly decomposed, there may be diseases and bacteria lurking in this rich mix that are deadly to seedlings. The mixture above is safer and also helps to stretch your compost further. To make sure your seed-bed soil is finely textured, sift it through a screen mesh before filling

  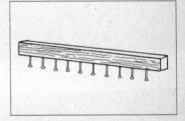

LEFT: *If you are making your own seed-bed soil, it's a good idea to build a wood-frame sieve using ¹/₄-inch hardware cloth for the metal grid. This allows you to fill flats directly from the sieve, ensuring soil that is light and free of rocks, sticks, and hard dirt clods.* RIGHT: *Once the seed is in place, it's essential that you cover it with the right amount of soil. Very small seed may require only ¹/₁₆ inch of soil to cover it, which is difficult to do by hand. Simplify this by filling an old mayonnaise jar with cover soil. Poke holes in the lid with a nail and screw it onto the jar. Then simply shake out the soil as you would salt, in a thin but much more even layer.*

To make evenly spaced depressions in a seed bed, create a guideline bar. Use a 2-by-2-inch wood segment to create a bar from 12 to 18 inches long. Pound a series of nails into the bar securely at regular intervals. If you then turn it over with the nails facing downward and press it gently into a flat of soil, you'll be able to space your seeds more accurately.

your containers. This is simply a 2-by-4-inch frame with a tightly stretched metal screen mesh attached. Grids should be about $1/4$- or $1/8$-inch hardware cloth, which can be purchased at any hardware store. The screen used to cover foundation vents for houses is ideal. Mix the sand, soil, and compost separately before passing it through the screen. Discarded colanders and kitchen sieves also work well if they have big holes.

SIMPLE STEPS TO SUCCESSFUL SEED GERMINATION

1. Buy or mix seed-growing soil that is finely textured and light.
2. If you have pottery shards, pea gravel, or very coarse sand, place a layer of this in the bottom of the containers to help with drainage.
3. Use only clean, well-sifted seed-bed soil without woody materials.
4. Plant the seed at the exact depth indicated on the package. Use a seedling-bed marker to create rows or an even grid.
5. Cover seed with a light material, such as compost, that won't pack down. Sift it through a kitchen strainer or poke holes in the top of a mayonnaise jar to create a "salt shaker" for cover soil.
6. Water with a misting nozzle to avoid dislodging seed or its covering.

Another method is to set the red clay pot in another larger container filled with water to just below the rim and let it soak through the porous clay until the soil is thoroughly moistened.

COLD FRAMES AND HOT BEDS— THE POOR GARDENER'S GREENHOUSE

A cold frame is no more than a glass-topped wooden box that insulates seedlings or cuttings from extreme temperature and dehydration. Anyone serious about gardening should have one, as it is far better suited to the backyard than a greenhouse. The best kind of top is simply a glass window, preferably one in a wooden frame, but aluminum is fine too. It can be a single sheet of glass, but these tend to break easily; if they're not tempered, this can be very dangerous. That's why many

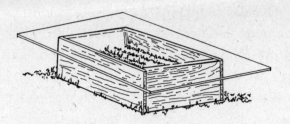

LEFT: This is one of the simplest ways to create a cold frame for germinating seed or encouraging cuttings to root. It consists of a wooden box with a sheet of glass set directly on top. A good place to obtain glass is from an automobile wrecking yard. Windows from junked cars are tempered, which is much safer, because if the glass breaks it disintegrates into small pieces rather than large sharp fragments. RIGHT: This traditional cold frame utilizes a six-pane window attached to a wooden box with a hinge. Notice how the top of the box is slanted. This allows more direct sunlight to reach the interior, and ideally this slant should face south.

people prefer a window that contains a series of smaller glass panes. *It's a lot easier to get the window first and build the box to fit it than the other way around.*

The box can be made from a framework of 2-by-4s and the outside covered with planks or plywood. The window should be attached to the rear wall with stout hinges and screws—not nails, which pull out easily as the wood shrinks and swells when you water. The dimensions of a cold frame are not rigid, but because the wooden frames, or sashes, of very large windows tend to lose their strength over time, the average cold frame is not larger than 3 feet wide by 5 to 6 feet long. It is usually located where it receives a full southern exposure.

For real tightwads, there's yet another way to create a temporary cold frame: using bales of straw instead of a wooden box. Straw bales are strong enough to stand up on their own and provide incredible insulation. Gardeners in far northern climates are building straw-bale houses, sheds, and greenhouses by stacking bales and driving metal-reinforcing rods into the straw to connect each course of bales. It is important, however, that these straw-bale structures be sealed against dampness, because the bacteria inside fermenting wet bales can cause spontaneous combustion. For more information on straw-bale construction, refer to David Bainbridge's book *The Straw Bale House* ($25, Chelsea Green Publishing).

A temporary straw-bale cold frame need only be one or two courses tall with a large window placed on top. For best results the cold-frame window should face south and the surface should be slanted by using a single course of bales in front and a double course for the back wall. Metal sash sliding glass doors are ideal for a cold frame because they must, by law, be tempered and are big enough to make a small greenhouse. When the weather warms, break open the bales to use as mulch on the summer garden.

"Hotbed" is another term linked to cold frames. They are basically the same thing except the hotbed is deeper. Cuttings strike roots and seeds germinate better if heat is applied to the bottom of their containers. Old-time gardeners used to place a thick layer of fresh manure in the bottom of their hotbeds, then cover it with soil or wood upon which their seed containers were placed. The manure heats up naturally because of biotic decomposition, as with the interior of a compost

English gardeners developed this method of creating miniature portable greenhouses out of picture frames or small windows of similar size. These are used for propagation and to shelter seedlings in spring or fall.

TOP: *In order to make the portable picture-frame greenhouse more sturdy, simply create a crossbar out of wood and secure it, as shown, to two nails.* MIDDLE: *To use automobile windows or glass that lacks a wood or metal frame, lash together sticks, which will support the glass. Lean each pane up against the incline, with the bottom resting directly on the soil. If the edges of the glass are sharp, simply cover them with protective duct tape to make handling safer.* BOTTOM: *Here's another way to support two similar-sized panes of unframed glass. The 3-by-5-inch block of wood simply clips the tops together. This method may be difficult to make if you're not used to working with wood.*

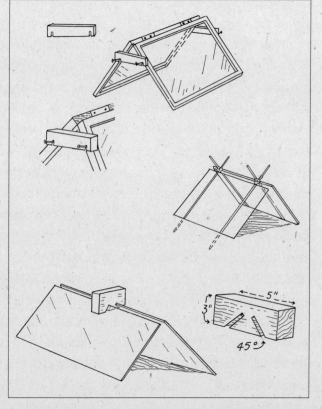

pile, and because heat always rises, it warms the hotbed from the bottom. The added warmth is important in climates where spring comes late and where simply enclosing the seed beds with a cold frame is not enough to encourage early germination.

PROTECTING SEEDLINGS FROM LATE-SPRING COLD SNAPS

To create a simple seedling protector, cut the bottom off a plastic half-gallon or gallon milk jug. Poke holes in the lid or remove it entirely to ensure that there is sufficient oxygen.

When that little seedling is transplanted out into garden soil, it will experience less-than-ideal conditions. Winds, whether cold or hot, can dry foliage and can even snap off the stems. Hungry pests seeking the greens of spring chomp these babies before they have a chance to grow. Unexpected late frosts can wither them in a single night. These problems afflict every gardener, and over the years there have been many ingenious attempts to resolve the problems. Gardening books recommend all sorts of bed coverings you can *buy*—but there are better ways to do it free.

From wartime England comes an ingenious way to protect seedlings from cold and even snow. Don't pass up the battered picture frames at your next garage sale if they still contain the glass. Take two frames of about the same size and attach them along one side with a hinge or two, like book binding. Place this miniature A frame over a row of seedlings. It is self-supporting and can be removed easily as soon as the little plants are on their way. It's also a great way to protect them from being crushed by a late snow.

One trick developed primarily for cuttings is the use of bell jars. These were actually blown-glass, bell-shaped jars that were set down over the cutting. They are expensive and rare, but a wide-mouth quart Mason jar is a good substitute. For longer cuttings, try a half-gallon Mason jar. Better yet, inquire at local delis and restaurants for their leftover jars. Pickles, olives, pig's feet, and other products are frequently packed into gallon-size or larger jars, which are precious commodities to the gardener. Get some of these jars even if you have to pay for them. They are versatile and can also be used to protect seedlings planted early in spring from occasional frost.

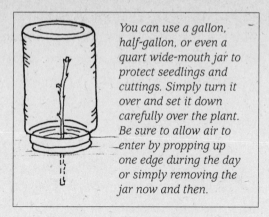

You can use a gallon, half-gallon, or even a quart wide-mouth jar to protect seedlings and cuttings. Simply turn it over and set it down carefully over the plant. Be sure to allow air to enter by propping up one edge during the day or simply removing the jar now and then.

Since seedlings tend to be small, you can cut the bottom off a plastic milk jug and cover them with a free portable greenhouse. Beware, however, that they don't become overheated and starved for oxygen during the warmer parts of the day. You can put the little greenhouses on in the evening and remove them in the morning, or remove the milk-jug cap for better air exchange.

Another great insulator is drafting Mylar, which can be used in lieu of thinner plastic sheeting for cold frames, row covers, or wind shields. It is a thick, semitransparent film used for mapping and engineering plans. It is far heavier than Mylar used for kites or balloons. You'd be amazed at how much of it goes into the garbage cans at architect or engineering offices, city or county planning departments, and aerial-mapping companies. If you pay them a visit and express your interest in scrap Mylar, they will probably be glad to give you all you can handle.

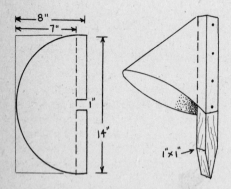

CONE PLASTIC PLANT COVER
Cut Mylar or similar stiff plastic into a semicircle, as shown here. Attach it to a 1-by-1-inch wood stake to create an adjustable temporary protective cover.

Pieces can be as large as 4 feet wide by 7 or 8 feet and occasionally even longer. There will probably be lines drawn or photographed on the Mylar, although occasionally you might score a good clean piece. To remove ink lines that are water-soluble, simply scrub the Mylar with a damp sponge. Photo-emulsion lines, usually on the back side of the sheet, are more difficult to remove but will come off with fine-grit sandpaper or when scraped with a knife.

Mylar also comes in handy for making cone-shaped plant coverings, which can be reused numerous times. Simply cut a circle 14 inches in diameter in the Mylar, then cut that in half and roll the half into a cone. This can be nailed or stapled to an anchor stake and pressed into the soil beside the seedling. It helps block wind and diffuse sunlight and can be raised or lowered to control air movement.

Another good way to block wind and retain some heat is with waxed milk or ice-cream cartons or larger tin cans with the top and bottom removed. These are too slick for pests such as cutworms to get over easily, and they can be left on all the time. If you duct-tape a piece of Mylar over the top of these cartons or can tubes, they stay much warmer, but the Mylar will need to be removed occasionally to allow air circulation. If you find removing the Mylar too inconvenient, punch a few small holes in the top.

Other types of large-scale coverings can extend harvesttime well into the fall. The simplest method is a Quonset-style covering made of $\frac{1}{2}$-inch-diameter lengths of PVC pipe. The ends of the pipe are pushed into the soil to create an arch. A series of them can be set up in a row and sheet plastic can then be laid over the top

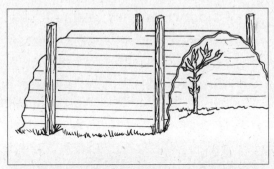

CORRUGATED PLASTIC ROW-CROP COVER
To extend the harvest from your vegetable crops, stake a panel of corrugated fiberglass roofing in place as shown. It is surprisingly durable and will stand up under light snowfall. Later in the fall, you can store these corrugated strips flat and out of the way under the house, beneath decking, or up on rafters in the garage. You may find used segments of this material at house-demolition yards, or simply buy it new at a home-improvement store.

STRAW BALE ROW-CROP COVER
In the Midwest, avid gardeners rely on greenhouses for their winter veggies. Many have created entire structures of stacked straw bales that are plastered with stucco on the outside. Not only are they thick, sturdy, and inexpensive, but the insulation factor is considerable as well. In a simplified version of this idea, straw bales are stacked into two walls and thick plastic sheeting or corrugated fiberglass roofing panels are laid over the top. The following season, you can till the straw into the garden or use it as a surface mulch.

and anchored with duct tape, or the ends can be buried in trenches. A simpler method uses cheap plastic corrugated panels manufactured as skylights for corrugated steel roofing—commonly found in home-improvement stores. These bend easily and are much stronger than the arch-and-sheet-plastic combination. They are also less vulnerable to snow and wind than plastic sheeting, which tends to tear under pressure.

GROWING NEW PLANTS FROM CUTTINGS

The majority of trees, shrubs, and vines and some perennials sold at nurseries are vegetatively propagated from cuttings. This process is simple in concept: cut off a part of one plant, make it grow roots, and replant it somewhere else. There are so many different types of plants, however, that whole books deal with nothing but the peculiar preferences and limitations of propagating various species from cuttings. More advanced gardeners who want to pursue this method more extensively should purchase one of the many reference books available today on plant propagation.

Since the number of methods of this kind of propagation is so vast, just a few of the easiest methods will be included here, as a sort of crash course. First of all you must understand how plants develop roots. Cuttings are composed entirely of stem cells, which are incapable of sending out roots because roots are composed of a different type of cell. The plant must develop an intermediate type of tissue called "callus," which is neither stem nor root but a type of growth from which the first root cells are produced. The period of time required for callus formation varies with each species. Woody cuttings can take an entire winter before the white, scablike callus tissue is fully visible. That's why hardwood cuttings take so much longer to root than softwood cuttings, which may produce roots in a matter of weeks.

Science has produced a synthetic hormone to help plants root more quickly from cuttings. When this powder is applied to the end of a cutting, the plant need not produce its own hormone to dictate a change of tissue type. You'll find rooting hormones at a garden center under various trade names, such as Rootone. It's definitely worth the price if you're planning to propagate plants from cuttings.

TIGHTWAD GARDENING TIP: The chief enemy of cuttings is inadequate drainage. Just because the container has a hole in the bottom doesn't mean a plant is adequately drained. The potting soil in the bottom of most containers can become highly saturated and rot if there is a lot of organic matter that absorbs and holds water. The best way to make sure you don't encounter this problem, whether growing seeds or newly rooted cuttings, is to line the bottom of each container with pebbles, pottery shards, charcoal chunks, or anything else you have that does not absorb water or rot. Make the thickness of this layer up to 30 percent of the entire contents of the pot.

TYPES OF CUTTINGS

Cuttings are divided into two main types: softwood or hardwood. These terms indicate the state of the plant tissue when the cutting was taken and the part of the mother plant where it originated. Many plants are suited to *both* softwood or hardwood cuttings, so if you aren't successful with one method, try the other.

SOFTWOOD CUTTINGS

These are taken during the summer, while the plant tissue is still green and soft. Summer tissue is rapidly growing and more inclined to root, but it is also vulnerable to dehydration. Most houseplant cuttings you see rooting in water on windowsills are good examples of softwood cuttings. Many perennials and evergreen shrubs are also propagated this way. Softwood cuttings require plenty of warmth, preferably a constant temperature without cold snaps, which is easier to maintain in northern climates, during the summer months. An old test for the quality of a softwood cutting states that if it is right, "the shoot will *snap clean across* instead of bend or only partially break; if it bends, it is too old."

The ideal size of your cutting is from 3 to 6 inches long, depending on the plant. It's best to remove all but a few leaves at the top to help speed up the rooting process. Apply your rooting hormone to the cut stub according to the instructions

SOME GARDEN PLANTS TYPICALLY GROWN FROM SOFTWOOD CUTTINGS

Genus	Common Names	Plant Type
Abelia	Abelia	Shrub
Abutilon	Flowering maple	Perennial
Aubrieta	Aubrieta	Perennial
Azalea	Azalea	Shrub
Begonia	Begonia	Perennial
Cactus	Cactus	Succulent
Calceolaria	Lady's purse	Perennial
Camellia	Camellia	Shrub
Chrysanthemum	Chrysanthemum	Perennial
Cistus	Rockrose	Shrub
Cytisus	Broom	Shrub
Dianthus	Pinks, carnation	Perennials
Erica	Heather	Shrub
Escallonia	Escallonia	Shrub
Forsythia	Forsythia	Shrub
Geranium	Geranium	Perennial
Grevillea	Grevillea	Shrub
Fuchsia	Fuchsia	Perennial
Hibiscus	Rose of Sharon	Shrub
Hydrangea	Hydrangea	Shrub
Hypericum	St. John's wort	Perennial
Ilex	Holly	Shrub
Jacaranda	Jacaranda	Tree
Jasminum	Jasmine	Vine
Kerria	Lavender starflower	Shrub
Lantana	Lantana	Perennial
Lavandula	Lavender	Perennial
Leptospermum	New Zealand tea tree	Shrub
Mahonia	Oregon grape	Shrub
Myrtus	Myrtle	Shrub
Nerium	Oleander	Shrub
Pelargonium	Geranium	Perennial
Penstemon	Beard tongue	Perennial
Phlox	Phlox	Perennial
Poinsettia	Poinsettia	Perennial/shrub
Rosa	Rose	Shrub
Salvia	Sage	Perennial
Scabiosa	Pincushion flower	Perennial
Sedum	Stonecrop	Succulent
Spiraea	Bridalwreath	Shrub
Succulents	Succulents	Perennials

Genus	Common Names	Plant Type
Syringa	Lilac	Shrub
Trachelospermum	Star jasmine	Vine
Verbena	Verbena	Perennial
Viburnum	Snowball	Shrub

on the package, then insert the cuttings into your rooting medium. Stiff stems can simply be pushed down into the sand, leaving one or two nodes and the leaves aboveground. If stems are soft, use a dibble or a piece of wood such as a pencil to push a clean hole in the sand. Gently place the cutting at the correct depth and tamp the sand down around it.

Since these softwood cuttings were actively growing when they were taken, they will lose moisture quickly. They should be well shaded and kept evenly moist, but not so wet that drainage is compromised or fungus growth appears. If allowed to wilt from lack of moisture, the cutting may never recover. Protection from cold night air is important as well, since most cuttings will root at temperatures from 55° to 65° F., and tropical species demand even warmer conditions. If cuttings be-

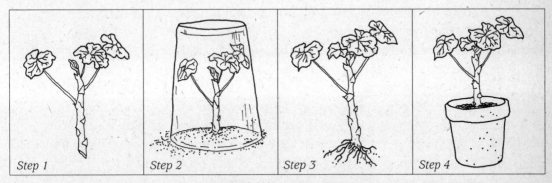

| Step 1 | Step 2 | Step 3 | Step 4 |

ROOTING A GERANIUM

Geraniums are one of the simplest perennials to root from a softwood cutting. Step 1—Take a tip cutting and remove all but the top few leaves. Step 2—Insert the cutting into the rooting medium and cover with an inverted glass or plastic container to reduce dehydration. Be sure to allow sufficient oxygen to enter by removing this cover every day. Step 3—After two weeks, check the cutting frequently for signs of root development. When a number of new roots are showing, it is ready to be planted into soil. Step 4—Plant the newly-rooted cutting in a flowerpot and keep moist until ready to plant outdoors. Be sure to acclimate new plants to outdoor conditions gradually to avoid shock.

gin to grow vigorously, gradually remove the shading or they will become weak and spindly. Softwood cuttings should produce roots in one week to one month, depending on the species. Check the progress frequently by gently digging out a cutting, and when it shows signs of rooting, it's time to transplant. Remember, the sand medium contains virtually no nutrition, so if the cuttings are to continue growing they must be moved into fertile soil.

HARDWOOD CUTTINGS

Except for roses, this method of propagation is not well suited to beginner gardeners. Hardwood cuttings are typically from one-year-old wood that is strong and firm

STEALING SUCCULENTS AND CACTI

The family of succulents such as iceplant, sedum, cacti, and others are by far the easiest plants of all to grow from cuttings. Succulents, which store their high water content in thick, fleshy leaves, have the unique ability to remain viable for a long time after being severed from the mother plant. In fact, the prickly pear cactus paddles can live for *two years* after being cut and still retain enough energy to grow. Cacti and succulents purchased by mail order are typically shipped as bare roots.

This viability prompts people who propagate their own cacti and succulents to be garden thieves, breaking off tiny pieces here and there to secrete away in a pocket. Beware of cacti, as they have vicious thorns, and the seemingly soft, fuzzy ones are particularly deadly. Once these small thorns get stuck in a pocket, you'll regret it every time you reach in to fish something out. It's better to be well prepared for cacti stealing with a pair of barbecue tongs, gloves, and lots of newspaper to wrap each piece in separately. Keep thorny cuttings separated from one another, as the thorns will puncture the fleshy part of any other cutting they touch. Wounds of this sort weaken the plants through moisture loss and increase the potential for rot to set in.

continued

Succulents and cacti root in gravel, sand, or virtually anything else that is well drained. Since these plants tend to be moist and fleshy, most will rot if placed directly into standing water or if a wet wound is introduced to a moist rooting medium. Try to break off the cutting at a natural joint, and if the wound does not dry out by the time you're ready to plant, then set it aside for another day or two. Succulents can strike roots in a matter of days, and once they are established, they produce an unlimited supply of new plants for your garden.

Make sure your rooting pot is fast-draining, and water only when the plants show the first signs of wilt or shriveling. You can dig down now and then to check for roots, and when they appear, you can transplant the cutting into the garden or a pot with more fertile but well-drained soil. A good rule of thumb for gauging potting-soil drainage suitable for cacti and succulents is: If you fill the pot to the rim with water, it should drain through in 15 seconds or less. If not, then drainage is insufficient and you need a more porous mix.

SUCCULENTS

LEFT: *This popular succulent,* Echeveria elegans, *is known affectionately as hens and chicks. The name was derived from the plant's habit of developing plantlets around the mother plant that look like baby chicks peeking out from beneath a sitting hen. This growth habit makes the plant easy to propagate—you simply break or cut off the baby plants with as much stem and root attached as possible. The new plants will root rapidly in damp sand and in a short time can be planted out in the garden.* CENTER: *Prickly pear cactus is a member of the genus* Opuntia, *which is propagated by simply breaking off a paddle-shaped leaf and nestling it in moist sand or directly into garden soil. Remove any fruit or flowers, since these will draw growth energy from the developing roots.* RIGHT: *Christmas cactus is an indoor succulent in all but the warmest states and is equally easy to propagate. Break off the growing tip at a natural joint in the leaves for a two-to-three-segment cutting. Place end in moist sand.*

SOME GARDEN PLANTS TYPICALLY PROPAGATED BY HARDWOOD CUTTINGS

Genus	Common Name	Plant Type
Berberis	Barberry	Shrub
Bougainvillea	Bougainvillea	Shrub/vine
Buxus	Boxwood	Shrub
Camellia	Camellia	Shrub
Celtis	Hackberry	Tree
Cornus	Dogwood	Tree
Chaenomeles	Quince	Tree/Shrub
Euonymus	Euonymus	Shrub
Hydrangea	Hydrangea	Shrub
Ilex	Holly	Shrub/tree
Jacaranda	Jacaranda	Tree
Jasminum	Jasmine	Vine
Kerria	Lavender starflower	Shrub
Lavandula	Lavender	Shrub/perennial
Lagerstroemia	Crape myrtle	Tree/shrub
Ligustrum	Privet	Shrub
Lonicera	Honeysuckle	Vine
Mahonia	Oregon grape	
Morus	Mulberry	Tree
Nerium	Oleander	Shrub
Populus	Poplar	Tree
Puncia	Pomegranate	Tree
Rhododendron	Azalea	Shrub
Rosa	Rose	Shrub
Salix	Willow	Tree
Spiraea	Bridalwreath	Shrub
Syringa	Lilac	Shrub

and shows no sign of withering. Growers take their cuttings in the fall before the ground freezes, placing them into deep wooden boxes filled with coarse sand for the winter, where the cuttings callus in time for planting in spring. Some save space by bundling up a handful of cuttings and binding them with a thick rubber band before burying in sand. In spring the callused cuttings are lifted from the sand and planted out in garden soil or in pots, where they begin producing roots as temperatures warm.

The size of a hardwood cutting can vary from a few inches to a full foot in length, with diameters averaging about the size of a pencil. Cuttings must have at

MIRACLE PLANTS THAT ROOT ON THEIR OWN

Despite the difficulties discussed above, some woody plants are very quick to produce roots. These are primarily trees and shrubs, such as willows and poplars, that grow along riverbanks and are fibrous-rooted, meaning they have very dense networks of relatively small roots. If you were to cut a long sucker from a willow or poplar and lay it down upon the ground and secure it, the entire side in contact with the soil would send out roots, and the opposite side would produce a row of shoots! There is no reason to buy any of these plants if there are other mature specimens in the neighborhood. If you want a weeping willow, for example, contact the owner and ask if you can take a few cuttings. Once it is established in your garden, you are assured an unlimited number of cuttings for future use.

The best time to plant poplar and willow cuttings is during winter, when the branches are leafless, so that growth begins with the onset of spring. To plant them, simply push the bottom end of the cutting into moist soil or into a post hole, fill it in, and keep the ground evenly damp. Before long it will produce branches and leaves, growing at an astounding rate of more than 5 feet per year. Use this method obtain weeping willow, corkscrew willow, pussy willow, Lombardy poplar, cottonwood, aspen, most species of alder, elms, and other water-loving trees as well.

Pussy willows, with their silver buds, are popular in floral displays. Combine interior decorating with propagation by cutting some whips in late winter and placing them in a deep jug of water indoors. Change the water every day or so, and pretty soon they'll send out roots. That's when you plant them outdoors.

least two buds, one for top growth and one for root development, but more buds are recommended to compensate for losses or damage. Be aware of exactly which end is up on your hardwood cuttings because they may not have any leaves when taken, and if planted upside down they do not root at all. Some growers cut the bottom of their cuttings on an angle to avoid confusion, also making it easier to insert them into the rooting medium. Don't be surprised if your first efforts at hardwood-cutting propagation are unsuccessful, as this is a learned skill.

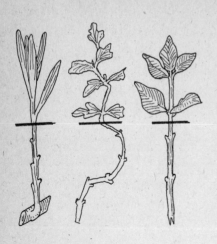

SOFTWOOD CUTTINGS
These are three examples of different types of softwood cuttings with leaves and stems removed from the underground portions. The lines show how deep the cuttings should sit in the rooting medium.

For simple and more successful propagation by cuttings, it's helpful to have either a greenhouse, a cold frame, a hotbed, or simply a box covered with glass, as shown on page 69. Cuttings of all sorts root far better when there is heat *beneath* their rooting medium. This makes the hotbed ideal, because the layer of warm manure set underneath will provide warmth.

The budget gardener will discover that mild bottom heating will occur if you place your rooting containers on a shelf above a heater vent, wood stove, or kitchen stove. Unless protected by a greenhouse-like environment, however, the cuttings, particularly leafy softwood cuttings, can be prematurely dried by such rising heat. You may want to cover your cuttings with a layer of plastic, to create a greenhouse-like environment inside your home.

ROOTING MEDIUM

The key to making a cutting root quickly is to use a quality rooting medium with rapid drainage. Cuttings, especially softwood cuttings, must be kept consistently moist but not so wet that they rot. In warm weather or when bottom heat is applied, the medium may require watering virtually every day to ensure that the plant tissue does not become the least bit dehydrated. The rooting process requires plenty of oxygen in the medium as well. Do not use garden soil as a rooting medium, because with its slow drainage it's likely to become oversaturated and oxygen-starved. In a very short time you could drown new roots or rot the cutting.

Propagators prefer *coarse* sand for rooting both softwood and hardwood cuttings. This is because the irregular-shaped fragments are not rounded, as beach sand is, and thus do not pack together as tightly. You can buy bagged rooting mediums, such as Pearlite and vermiculite, for cuttings as well, but these cost money and are not necessarily an improvement over sand.

Budget gardeners should stick to the original medium, coarse sand. You can buy it in bulk and use part for rooting and the rest for soil improvement elsewhere in the garden. In addition to the ways of finding sand described in Chapter 2, you'll find it with concrete and plaster supplies at the home-improvement store. Note that sandy deposits found on the banks of reservoirs or rivers or in flood plains will work, but the organic matter in this sand may foster damping off, a deadly disease that kills both seedlings and cuttings. Coarse construction sand tends to be more sterile and less likely to contain damping off. It's always a good idea to use fresh rooting medium with each crop of cuttings to avoid carrying damping off or other problems onto next year's plants.

Containers used for rooting cuttings must be more durable than those used to grow seedlings. This is because it can take many months before a cutting is well rooted and ready to plant in the garden, and all that time the rooting medium is quite damp. The most common type of container is a deep wooden box, which is used over and over by nursery propagators. An old wooden dresser drawer is ideal. Since drawers are sometimes glued, it's best to reinforce it with nails or metal brackets on the corners before filling with rooting medium. Without this extra support the constant moisture warps the wood separating the original corner joints and causing the entire box to fall apart. Another option is crisper drawers from old refrigerators. These are plastic or enameled tin and hold up forever, but you must be sure to puncture the bottom for drainage holes for any type of container that you use. Wooden drawers, crisper drawers, and a wide variety of other containers can be collected cheaply at the dump, junkyard, or house-demolition yard.

SOFTWOOD-CUTTING ROOTING CONTAINER This simple arrangement ensures that the rooting medium remains sufficiently moist without becoming too wet. Plug a clay flowerpot and set it into the rooting medium of a larger pot. Arrange cuttings around the edge as shown. Keep the flowerpot filled with water and it will gradually seep evenly into the surrounding medium.

It can be difficult for busy gardeners to keep their cutting beds evenly moist, particularly during the warmer months. Old-timers devised a simple container for softwood cuttings to solve this problem. They would find an old washtub or soup pot and a much smaller red clay pot that fitted inside easily with at least 2 inches clear on all sides. The bottom of the large pot was lined with shards or charcoal and then filled with coarse sand. The clay pot was buried in the sand to about 1 inch from its rim. You can shave down the cork from a wine bottle or a wax candle stub until it fits snugly in the drain hole at the bottom. Insert your cuttings into the ring of sand that now surrounds the little clay pot. To water, simply fill the clay pot, and gradually the moisture seeps through the sides into the sand. This may take hours or all day, depending on the size of the pot and the climate. If you were to water the sand directly, the water would simply flow through all at once and the rooting medium would dry out again.

LAYERING—A SAFE AND RELIABLE ALTERNATIVE TO HARDWOOD CUTTINGS

Layering is a method of propagation that allows you to root a portion of an existing plant easily and without risk, but it results in only one new plant per layer. It has been used in the past to propagate vines, since many of their runners will naturally root when they encounter the soil. Layering can be used on many other types of

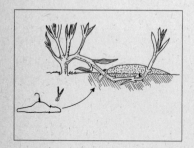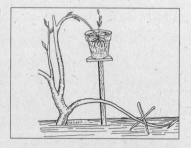

PROPAGATION BY LAYERING
Most vines or other plants that are sufficiently flexible can be propagated by layering. LEFT: *Step 1—Bend down a lower branch of your plant and place it in a small groove in the soil. Nick the bottom of the limb to encourage rooting and add hormones if you wish. Anchor the limb in the soil with giant "bobby pins" made of coat hangers. Cover the remainder of the limb with sand or soft topsoil.* CENTER: *Step 2—Check the limb after a few weeks for signs of rooting. During warm months this may occur quickly, but during cold weather it can take many months. When the damaged portion begins to show sufficient rooting, cut it off the mother plant. Many believe you should sever the limb but wait a week before transplanting the newly rooted part because severing and transplanting at the same time can create unnecessary shock.* RIGHT: *Another method of layering allows you to place the new plant in a pot right from the start. Then when you sever it from the mother plant, there is no need for transplanting.*

ORNAMENTALS THAT TAKE TO LAYERING

Botanical genus	Common name
Chrysanthemum	Chrysanthemum
Cistus	Rockrose
Cotoneaster	Cotoneaster
Clematis	Clematis
Dianthus	Carnations
Echium	Pride of Madeira
Hoya	Wax vine
Laburnum	Golden chain tree
Lonicera	Honeysuckle
Mandevilla	Mandevilla
Nerium	Oleander
Parthenocissus	Boston ivy
Pyracantha	Firethorn
Robinia	Locust
Rosa	Climbing/species roses
	All berry vines

plants as well, and for the beginner this is an ideal way to increase garden plants with little risk.

If you were to study berry vines or some of the larger chrysanthemums, you'd notice that their long flexible limbs tend to lie down upon the soil if not staked upright. When this happens, the branch becomes covered with litter, and if it is sufficiently moist it is likely to send out roots wherever soil contact occurs. Layering does exactly the same thing, but you must help it along by pegging the branch and mounding rooting medium around that point.

To layer a plant, select a long branch that can come in contact with the soil and still have enough left at the tip to start a new plant. Some propagators scrape or even break the bottom side of the branch to speed things up, because the plant will develop callus tissue in the effort to heal. You can add rooting hormone to that point as well. Once you've placed the branch on the soil, peg it with giant "bobby pins" made of wire coat hangers. Mound sand or compost about 3 to 4 inches over the break and leave it for a month or two, or even all winter. Species that tend to layer themselves naturally may root in a few weeks, while less-inclined plants may take months. But since you don't have to worry about dehydration or bottom heat, you can layer it and forget it. Once the roots have developed, the branch leading to the mother plant can be severed. If you want to transplant the new plant, wait a few days to allow it to get used to being separated from the mother plant.

Most vines, with their flexible runners, can be propagated by layering, but plants with stiff upright limbs make poor candidates. Layering is the best way to obtain vines or berry plants. Because they take to this method so eagerly, you need only buy one plant. You can layer it during the first season into a whole batch of new ones.

DIVISION OF PLANTS

Over time, many plants increase in size and benefit from division, which renews them and improves flower quantity and size. Dividing rewards budget gardeners with many new plantlets, roots, and bulbs, which should be potted and nurtured to the maximum number of healthy new plants.

PERENNIALS

When you buy a perennial, you are really buying many plants in one. As most perennials mature, they develop into larger and larger clumps with new plantlets popping up around the outside. The savvy budget gardener can separate these plantlets and transplant them elsewhere to develop into their own clumps. Perennials that lend themselves to this method are more valuable than those that cannot be easily divided. Daylilies, for example, can be dug up and divided in spring or in early autumn into dozens of new plants. Eventually a single daylily mother plant can populate an entire garden. The key is knowing the correct time of year to divide each species.

Prior to division the plant must be dug up. The safest tool for this is a spading fork, which will pull the roots gently rather than severing them as a shovel will. You can use two spading forks on either side of the plant, inverting them into the ground so that the lever action pops the plant out of the ground with the least amount of root damage. Once the plant is out of the soil, wash the roots off until they are clean enough to work with. Many plants will naturally fall apart at this

PERENNIALS THAT ARE EASILY DIVIDED

Botanical Genus	Common Name	Season for Division
Achillea	Yarrow	Fall
Agapanthus	Lily of the Nile	Early spring
Anemone	Anemone	After flowering
Armeria	Thrift	After flowering
Asparagus	Asparagus	Spring
Bamboos	Bamboo	Spring
Bellis	English daisy	After flowering
Chrysanthemum	Chrysanthemum	Fall or spring
Coreopsis	Coreopsis	Spring
Delphinium	Larkspur	Early spring
Dicentra	Bleeding heart	Early spring
Ferns	Ferns	Spring
Geum	Geum	Early spring
Hemerocallis	Daylily	Spring or fall
Heuchera	Coral bells	Spring
Kniphofia	Red hot poker	Early spring
Lupinus	Hybrid lupin	Early spring
Nepeta	Mint	Early spring
Oenothera	Evening primrose	Fall or spring
Rudbeckia	Black-eyed susan	Fall or spring
Salvia	Sage	Fall or spring
Thymus	Thyme	Fall or spring
Vinca	Periwinkle	Early spring

point. If the plant has lots of woody stuff in the center and many other smaller rooting units around it, discard the woody core and save the rest.

When out of the ground the plant is vulnerable and the pieces should be replanted or potted as quickly as possible so the roots don't dry out. Very small, weak segments can be planted in pots and nurtured through the winter before replanting outdoors in spring. Vigorous varieties, such as the Shasta daisy, may be planted into garden soil immediately after dividing the mother plant.

Knowing which plants are easiest to divide and the time of year to do so is important to their survival. A book on perennial plants is the best resource for the exact needs and limitations of most plants suitable for division. The month in which this task should be done will vary with local climates. Early spring typically means after the very first signs of growth. Fall or spring division takes advantage of transition times between dormancy and peak growth periods. Other species must be divided *after* they flower in order to avoid sacrificing that year's bloom.

Bulbs, Tubers, and Rhizomes

BULBS

Bulbs are one of the easiest plants to propagate, because during the growing season they develop bulblets around the mother bulb. Some, such as the gladiola, must be dug up and the little bulbs separated if they are to bloom well the following year. When daffodils are planted for naturalizing, they usually remain in the soil permanently and develop large colonies. But if they were dug up, they could be divided and replanted elsewhere successfully.

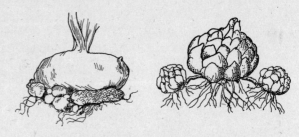

DIVIDING GLADIOLAS AND LILIES
LEFT: *Corms and true bulbs develop babies around their fleshy root structures each year. If they are dug up and split off, you can create many new plants. The babies may require a year or two of tender loving care to develop into blooming adults.* RIGHT: *Lilies develop long roots, which support new baby bulbs. When the lilies are dug up for winter, simply sever the long roots to free the new babies and nurture them for a season or two until they mature into entirely new plants.*

It's simple to divide bulbs. Do not dig them up until the foliage dies back on its own. Once you take them out of the ground, separate off the little bulbs and set them aside. The remaining mature bulbs may be stored until planting time or replanted immediately, depending on the species or type. When it's time to plant bulbs in your climate, the bulblets can go into a nursery bed or into pots to be nurtured through their first growing season. The large mother bulbs can be dug up again the following year or alternating years, depending on the type.

TUBERS

There are other fleshy rooted plants that aren't technically bulbs but tubers. The most well-known tuber is the potato, which sprouts from eyes in a fleshy root. Tubers are usually quite productive—a single original will produce many offspring

DIVIDING A DAHLIA TUBER.
It's easy to divide your dahlias into many new plants. First, dig up the cluster of tubers that surrounds the roots and store it until spring. Then sever each one very carefully so it has a portion of the stem attached that bears an eye. The eye is the source of next year's plant, and any tuber cut without a growth eye will fail to develop. Replant each of the severed tubers in spring.

over its life span. The most notable ornamental tuber is the dahlia, which develops a cluster of fleshy roots shaped like small sweet potatoes that all radiate out from a central point where the stem begins. In cold climates dahlia tubers must be dug up and stored for the winter. Division should be done in spring when it's time to plant. To divide the dahlia, you must carefully cut the tubers away from the central stalk with some stem attached, as this is where the growth eyes are located. Each tuber *must have an eye* or it simply won't grow.

RHIZOMES AND STOLONS

A rhizome is simply a long stem that travels underground to spread and create new plants. Runner grasses that invade gardens can travel quickly, because of their aggressive rhizome activity. A similar plant part, called the stolon, travels aboveground to create new plants. The best example is the strawberry, which vegetatively propagates itself by stolons. When a daughter plant (which is always smaller than the original plant) develops its own roots at the end of a stolon or rhizome, these may be severed and transplanted into new plants. Avid strawberry growers do this every year, following a three-year cycle of replacement for maximum yields.

The canna and bearded iris are two showy garden plants that grow from very stout, fleshy rhizomes. Huge old stands of cannas can be found in yards of older homes in more temperate states. Frequently they are considered weeds, and neighbors would be pleased if you dug some up. Look for cannas in neighborhoods of old Victorian homes—they were quite the rage back then. Cannas are not frost-hardy, so in cold winter climates the entire rhizome must be dug up at the end of the year and stored until spring. Older plants can develop such a large network of these roots that just digging them out will break them apart. In fact, these plants bloom a lot better after dividing, so it pays to propagate. For a divided canna root to be viable, it should be on the large side, with at least three buds.

> **CHEAP-SCAPES CHOICES:** Seas of daffodil bulbs are often one of the few lingering vestiges of long-forgotten homesteads. Those cultivars that do persist are often the most rugged and easy to grow and are resistant to gophers. If you find such botanical artifacts, contact the land owner and ask to dig up a few. It won't hurt the plants that remain and you can propagate your gleanings into a large family of your own.

Bearded iris are also called flags, after their tall flower stalks and exotic flowers. They are surprisingly tough and will grow in climates with minimal summer rainfall. Like cannas, they develop dense networks of fleshy roots that support blades of foliage. The time to divide them is during the summer after plants have ceased blooming and conditions are dry enough to discourage fungus and rotting of the fleshy roots. Since they lie at the surface of the soil, these plants are easy to dig. It's best to snap the rhizomes into segments rather than cutting them apart; let the wound harden off a day or two before replanting. Avoid planting too deep. The enormous number of different bearded iris hybrids and the range of spectacular colors make this plant excellent for trading among friends and neighbors.

DIVIDING BEARDED IRIS
To obtain many new plants from an overgrown patch of bearded iris, you must dig up the fleshy roots that sit just below the soil surface. Break apart each segment of root that bears a growing tip. Allow the cut ends a day or so to harden off before replanting, so there is less chance for moisture rot to set in. Be aware of just how shallow these roots were when you first dug them up and replant the new, smaller segments at a similar depth.

CHEAP-SCAPES CHOICES: Local gardening organizations become community clearinghouses for surplus plants and bulbs after members divide their plants. Anyone with a million yellow daylilies from the last few times they divided is likely to send the current fruits of division into the compost pile. But when gardeners get together and exchange their leftover plants, everybody benefits. Although garden clubs are not the rage they were earlier in this century, they are making a comeback for just this reason.

CHAPTER 6

SAVING ENERGY DOLLARS:

Gardening for More Comfortable Homes

Every time you switch on the heater or air conditioner in your house, it costs you money. In winter the bill is for electricity, oil, natural gas, propane, or cordwood. In summer it is electricity. If the year has been abnormally hot or cold, the bill skyrockets just to make the house livable. With the scheduled phase-out of refrigerants in the coming years, the efficiency of air conditioners and the costs to keep them operating will rise dramatically. This increases the value of energy-efficient landscaping, making it more important than ever before.

In recent years there has been extensive study of climate patterns in urban and suburban communities. A new term, "heat island," defines a problem that causes ambient air temperature to rise higher than normal because of the increased heat generated by hard surfaces. When the temperature is 100° out in the countryside, a nearby city might be 105° because of the accumulative heat radiating from building walls and paving. This is compounded by the fact that smog and other particulate matter in the air above cities create a barrier that prevents this superheated air from rising and dispersing into the atmosphere during the night as it should. So the heat accumulation can build up over many days or weeks instead of just during the day.

On the other hand, homes in colder climates suffer from icy winds that seek out every nook and cranny in a house's outer walls and can make outdoor spaces too cold to use even when the sun is shining. So great was the problem in the Midwest that as far back as the 1930s there was a concerted effort to develop windbreak planting concepts. Today these concepts have become the foundation of modern urban design to create similar protection in our cities.

Both of these examples illustrate how extremes of climate can make outdoor spaces less comfortable and increase the need for artificial heating and cooling indoors. Every homeowner or budget gardener can reduce the household fuel budget by deliberate selection and placement of landscape plants. Although it may take time for the plants to mature and become fully effective, in the long run they will make a big difference.

HOT-ZONE BASICS

GOAL: MAXIMIZE SUMMER SHADE, CONSERVE WINTER HEAT

Solar radiation is heat that reaches us from the sun. Your home receives this solar radiation, and depending on the type of exterior material you have, the walls will absorb and reflect this heat to a greater or lesser degree. A window facing west, subjected to the hot afternoon sun, will absorb a good amount of heat, then radiate it into the interior of the house. Perhaps the best example of this process is an auto sitting in the sun with all the windows rolled up. The heat passing through the glass is sufficient to bake the interior, which is why dashboards tend to crack and buckle. This can also happen through building walls, and homes with dark paint on the outer walls absorb a tremendous amount of heat, which transfers through to the interior. Double-pane windows and heavy wall insulation are two ways to reduce this problem, but they are very expensive to install in an existing home.

If you live in an old home, it is even more important that you landscape for energy conservation. Homes built before World War II usually have minimal insulation in the walls, floors, and ceilings. Tin or steel roofing can cause extremes of heat and cold beneath them. Wood sash windows dry, crack, and warp over time, developing openings around the edges, where cold winds enter. Planting for shade and wind screening will go a long way toward reducing your energy bills and making you more comfortable year-round without the expense of remodeling.

Solar radiation that falls upon plants is absorbed into the leaves and utilized in the process of photosynthesis. Therefore, well-placed trees function in two ways when they encounter solar radiation: They consume *and* intercept it before it reaches hard surfaces. Studies show that a mature shade tree can equal 10,000 BTUs of cooling by shading and absorption of solar radiation, and homeowners can expect to save an average of $73 per year in air-conditioning costs.

The cooling effects of landscaping are not limited to trees. Bare earth acts much like paving: It absorbs solar heat, then radiates it out into the atmosphere. But the same surface planted in lawn or ground cover will radiate very little heat. It stands to reason that the fewer paved surfaces and the more green foliage you arrange around your house, the less you'll be affected by summer's hot temperatures. Also, paving already in place but shaded by trees is less likely to radiate any appreciable heat.

What's Your Problem?

"Passive solar" is a term used by architects to describe building designs that take advantage of the sun without special mechanisms. Passive solar landscaping is similar, using plants rather than architecture to improve solar benefits. To cash in on outdoor passive solar landscaping, you must first look at your house and its orientation to the sun. Passive solar homes are oriented with the long side to the south, and these walls will have the greatest number of windows. Homes oriented to the street or the corners of a lot may not face directly south, and in these homes passive solar alteration is a little more difficult. In the Northern Hemisphere, the south side of your house receives the most sunlight during the winter months, when the sun is southerly in the sky. The west side takes the brunt of the hot afternoon summer sun and benefits the most from shading. You probably know this already, because certain rooms turn into hot boxes during the summer months. Shading is beneficial to walls as well as the roof, since high attic temperatures can radiate down into rooms through poorly insulated ceilings. That's why attic exhaust fans are so helpful in keeping homes cooler.

Trees should be clustered on the west side, because the hot afternoon sun is the most damaging during the summer. West-side and south-side trees must be "solar-

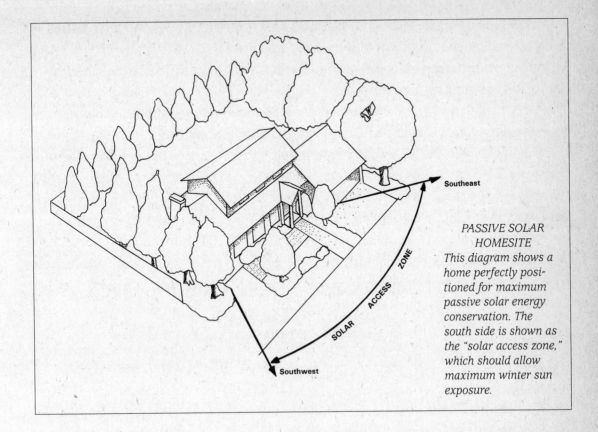

Southeast

SOLAR ACCESS ZONE

Southwest

*PASSIVE SOLAR
HOMESITE
This diagram shows a
home perfectly posi-
tioned for maximum
passive solar energy
conservation. The
south side is shown as
the "solar access zone,"
which should allow
maximum winter sun
exposure.*

friendly" species, which means they cool the house in summer but let the winter sun reach as much of the building as possible. Deciduous species such as maple and pin oak are solar-friendly because they automatically change with the season, going from leafy and shady in summer to bare, which allows sunlight to pass through their branches in winter.

In the very near future the federal government will be phasing out refrigerants due to their potentially detrimental effects on the ozone layer. There is a very real chance that air-conditioning as we know it today could suddenly become a scarce luxury. To prepare for this, it's wise to have shading trees as well as insulating shrubs and vines in place sooner, rather than later. The American Association of Nurserymen and the Garden Council have published studies comparing homes with and without shade trees. These studies show how useful and cost-effective shade trees are.

- Shaded houses uses 2.0 kilowatt hours per square foot per year, while unshaded houses use 3.3 KWH.
- One tree absorbs the same amount of BTUs in a given day as five air conditioners running for 20 hours.
- Walls shaded by trees are generally 15° F. cooler than unshaded walls.
- Shading your outdoor air-conditioning unit or evaporative cooler increases efficiency and the life of your equipment.

Given that trees can increase the overall value of your home by 5 to 20 percent, there are plenty of reasons to consider these options for your home.

HOW TO RECOGNIZE A SOLAR-FRIENDLY TREE

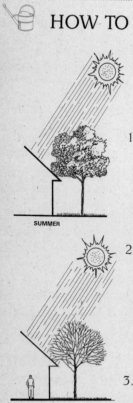

SOLAR-FRIENDLY TREES
Solar-friendly trees are deciduous, losing their leaves early in fall and growing them again in late spring. Deciduous trees provide shade during the heat of the summer, then stand bare during winter to allow light to shine through their branches.

1. Tree species that lose their leaves in *early fall* and grow them again in *late spring* maximize the period of time they stand bare during winter. In cold climates direct solar exposure is important early in the season, and when spring comes late, you don't have to have increased shade while it's still chilly outside.

2. Even after a tree has lost its leaves, the density of twigs and branches in the canopy can block sunlight. Canopy density varies with each species, from around 25 percent to as much as 80 percent. The average density is about 40 percent. A solar-friendly tree should have an open branching pattern, but existing trees with dense branching can be made more friendly by carefully pruning and thinning the canopy.

3. Seed pods and catkins that remain on trees during the winter increase the canopy density, as do tenacious leaves that may not detach as readily in some mild climates. Solar-friendly trees should have no such lingering parts.

TESTING FOR TREE-SHADOW PATTERNS

To get a better idea of how tall a tree is needed to shade your house, obtain a long pole and anchor it in the ground where you think the tree should be planted. Then watch its shadow pattern throughout the day to see exactly where shadows will fall. The shadow pattern is most important at midday during the hottest part of the summer, when shading provides the greatest benefit. The pole will also show you how the angle and length of the shadow at noontime differs with each season. This is a good way to study how the sun moves across the sky, and how changes in shadow from winter to summer affect exposures in different parts of the garden.

Another trick is used by architects to see how a building will look on a site, although this technique requires a perfectly calm day. First, they fill a number of large balloons with helium, then attach tails of kite string as long as the proposed building is tall. The strings are anchored to the ground with a weight where the building corners would be set. The balloons then rise to the proper height so the architects can stand way back to get a big picture of how their building will visually impact the surrounding area.

You can adapt this technique using a single balloon and a kite string 20 to 50 feet long, which is the average height of most shade trees. Anchor the string where you plan to put the tree and let the balloon rise. As the sun moves, over the course of the afternoon, you'll see exactly where the shadow will fall and how tall a tree is needed to do the job. To test more than one location or the width of the tree, simply use more balloons, then turn them over to the kids when you're through.

PICKING THE RIGHT TREE FOR YOU

The variety, size, and number of trees you use to shade your home depend on many factors. It's a good idea to consult a professional to help with selection of the tree to ensure that it is the proper species and not threatened by specific pests or diseases. Their knowledgeable assistance in exact placement also helps avoid any conflicts with both overhead and underground utilities, foundations, paving, and other existing features.

Not all trees have the same form or silhouette. A tree used for solar shading

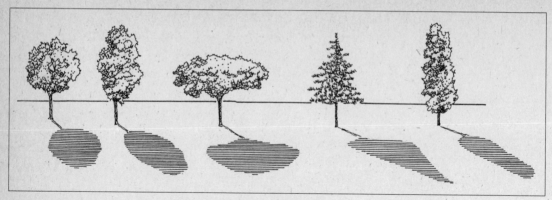

TREE SHADOW PATTERNS
Each species of tree has a certain form, which is reflected in the size and shape of its shadow pattern. This is an important factor in selecting solar-friendly trees that cast the proper shadow for reducing summer air-conditioning bills. Sometimes the more unusual shapes are ideal on small lots, where you must accurately place trees in order to avoid shading your neighbors' sunny south side. LEFT TO RIGHT: *round, vertical oval, horizontal oval, pyramidal, columnar.*

must have a broad canopy, like an open umbrella, rather than one that is columnar, like a baseball bat. Obviously the umbrella-shaped tree will give you far more bang for your buck when it comes to shading. Although a tree with greater canopy density improves summer shading, this must be weighed against the increased shading created by a bare but dense canopy in winter. In very cold winter climates, it's wise to avoid a tree with a dense canopy.

Above all, trees must be able to survive in your climate zone and should be both pest- and disease-resistant. Very fast growing trees, such as poplars, tend to have a short life span, something to keep in mind, since this tree won't cast an effective shade for many years. Avoid any of the very invasively rooted species, such as willows, poplars, maples, and alders, if you live on a small lot.

On small city lots, or where limited shading is needed, the simplest solution is to plant a single shade tree to intercept and absorb heat before it can reach the walls and windows. It must be a species that grows large enough to create a sufficient shade mass to shade not only the wall but a portion of the roof as well. It is unwise to plant trees right up against buildings, because the roots can damage foundations, and the canopy can interfere with roofing and rain gutters. The tree should be located at least 10 feet from the wall.

Purchasing solar-friendly trees for your homesite is an important task. To en-

sure that you have the correct species, accurately positioned, consult a master gardener or farm adviser, or hire a certified arborist or landscape architect. This is
money well spent. Don't fall for low-priced clearance trees. Saving a few dollars
now to plant the wrong species or a tree that is not healthy is a total waste and
eliminates any real benefit.

Trees and other plants are also beneficial because their transpiration, or breath-
ing process, expels both oxygen and moisture. When trees are planted together in
groves, the humidity among them can accumulate, adding yet another benefit:
evaporative cooling. This cooling effect is minimal when only one tree is present or
when trees are widely spaced. Using groves of trees to shade your home helps reduce the ambient outdoor air temperature, and it will be noticeably cooler in and
around the grove. In regions with high summer humidity, however, the evaporative
effect is not so pronounced, because of the existing moisture content in the air.

Trees planted in groves can shade a much larger portion of the house and roof.
Not only is a grove of trees larger in mass, but it is *deeper* and the overall density of
foliage is increased, limiting the amount of sun that passes through. In addition,
the increased shading of the soil beneath the tree grove reduces the amount of
heat absorbed and radiated by the earth. A grove also ensures that if one of the
trees dies, you won't lose all your shading.

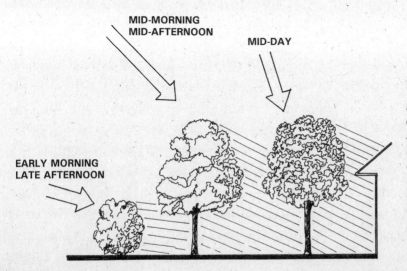

MID-MORNING
MID-AFTERNOON

MID-DAY

EARLY MORNING
LATE AFTERNOON

*BENEFITS OF
TREE GROVES
This diagram shows how
the angle of the sun
changes during the day. A
single tree may not be able
to provide all the shading
and protection you need,
but a combination of trees
and shrubs is much more
effective. A combination
creates a better environ-
ment for additional evaporative cooling as well.*

USING VINES FOR EXTERIOR INSULATION

It's difficult to add insulation inexpensively to the walls of an older house, but there is a cheap way to reduce radiant heat gain and loss through your walls. Just add insulation to the outside by planting vines, which can be trained to cover your house walls evenly. Their shading effect is considerable, and the dead air space between the vine foliage and the exterior wall is also a very effective insulator. Taller shrubs planted up against the house also provide the benefits of shading and insulating.

The simplest way to insulate walls with vines is to plant species that cling to the surface themselves. This makes it impossible to paint the house, however, and the vines can cause all sorts of unseen damage if not properly controlled. Vines that do not cling can be espaliered onto a simple grid trellis that is bolted to the wall. When it's time to paint the house, simply unbolt the trellis, or untie the vine from the trellis.

Vines are useful for shading windows, and they have been used this way for centuries in the hot climates of the Mediterranean and Latin America. In these arid regions the limited water supply leaves very little for plants, so those that are used for shading must have maximum effect. The most common procedure for shading with vines is to drape vine runners over the top of a window, where leafy shade blocks direct solar access to the home's interior. This also prevents heat transfer through glass windows when the sun is overhead. Bougainvillea and old roses were the most common types of vines used in the past, but virtually any plant with similar growth habits, such as Clematis and Honeysuckle, will suffice.

Draping vinelike plants over windows and doorways is much simpler than covering entire walls with a blanket of leaves. There are many species to choose from, some evergreen and others deciduous, which flower in a variety of hues. Clematis, climbing roses, trumpet vines, and jasmines all offer plenty of flowers and even fragrance. Deciduous vines won't block much of the sun, so the house won't be too dark during the short winter days. You can plant one vine per window or combine different types for a more varied flower color or to extend the bloom season. Train the vine directly up the side of your window, pruning it to one or two strong runners, then drape it across the top of the sash. These main runners will develop lateral branching, which makes the drape of the vine bushier and able to produce

DENSELY GROWING VINES FOR INCREASING WALL INSULATION

Botanical Name	Common Name	Evergreen	Clings	Hardy
Euonymus fortunei 'Colorata'	Wintercreeper	yes	yes	yes
Ficus pumila	Creeping fig	yes	yes	no
Hedera helix	English ivy	yes	yes	varies
Hydrangea anomala	Climbing hydrangea	no	yes	yes
Parthenocissus tricuspidata	Boston ivy	no	yes	yes
Parthenocissus quinquefolia	Virginia creeper	no	yes	yes
Wisteria sinensis	Chinese wisteria	no	no	yes
Wisteria floribunda	Japanese wisteria	no	no	yes

SHOWY FLOWERING VINES FOR DRAPING OVER WINDOWS

Botanical Name	Common Name	Evergreen	Hardy	Fragrant	Color
Bougainvillea hybrids	Bougainvillea	semi	no	no	many
Campsis radicans	Trumpet creeper	no	yes	no	red
Clematis hybrids	Clematis	no	yes	varies	many
Clytostoma callistegioides	Violet trumpet vine	yes	no	no	lavender
Distictus buccinatoria	Blood red trumpet vine	yes	no	no	red
Gelsemium sempervirens	Carolina jessamine	yes	no	yes	yellow
Jasminum polyanthum	Chinese jasmine	yes	no	yes	white
Lonicera spp	Honeysuckle	yes	varies	yes	pink/yellow
Passiflora x alatocaerulea	Hybrid passionflower	yes	no	no	white/purple
Rosa hybrid climbers	Climbing roses	no	varies	varies	many
Tecomaria capensis	Cape honeysuckle	yes	no	no	orange/yellow

Windspeed (MPH)	Actual Temperature (° F.)	Adjusted Wind-Chill Temperature (° F.)
5	20	17
10	20	5
15	20	−5
20	20	−10
25	20	−15

more flowers. Keep the vine neatly pruned and never allow it to grow beyond the reach of your ladder.

COLD-ZONE BASICS

Goal: Reduce winter winds, increase heat conservation

It is not difficult to understand how wind affects ambient temperatures in cold climates. The effect can be so great that temperatures are adjusted for "wind chill" in weather reports. On a typical 20° F. day, for example, the temperature will drop with each 5-mile-per-hour increase in wind speed. The wind chill factor is critical in determining the amount of energy required to heat a household during winter months.

The reason that down comforters and jackets are so warm is that down creates dead-air spaces in which body heat becomes trapped. The value of true goose down is that it remains fluffy, which helps support these air spaces inside each quilted cell of stuffing. But if down becomes wet, the fluff collapses and virtually all the insulation value disappears. Double-pane windows also have a layer of dead air sandwiched between the two sheets of glass. Dead air, or air that doesn't move, provides a valuable insulating barrier between areas of varying temperature.

DEAD AIR SPACE
Foundation planting is not just decorative but can serve a very important purpose as well—reducing energy consumption. Dense evergreen shrubs around the foundation of a house act as a windbreak to create dead air space.

Take this dead-air concept and apply it to a homesite. A barrier of dead air around your house will insulate its walls from direct contact with cold wind. Think of wind as you would water to better understand how it will impact your home. Wind cannot blow through your house, so it must split and go around the sides. This forces more direct contact with walls and windows on the sides that do not face the wind head-on. In many cases this detoured wind will eddy and swirl in many directions, which increases access to cracks in the walls or windows. You can wrap your home in evergreen foundation plantings or trained vines, which provide a dead-air space and hence a sizable and effective insulation blanket.

To plant for energy conservation, you must know how your prevailing winds and storm winds differ with each season. To find out, make a poor man's weather vane. Simply pound a tall (6 feet or over) stake or pole in the ground so it is sturdy enough to stand up to the wind. Then tie some strips of brightly colored cloth or ribbon securely to the stake at two-foot intervals. When the wind blows, the ribbons will point away from the source of the wind. For example, if the ribbons point east, then it's a west wind.

In order to block wind on a larger scale for energy conservation and to make outdoor spaces more comfortable, you must arrange a barrier of trees called a windbreak. A windbreak is basically a row of tightly spaced trees arranged in a line that runs perpendicular to the direction of the wind. For example, if you block a west wind, the windbreak must run north to south. Ideally the windbreak should be placed a distance from the home equal to two to four times the ultimate height of the windbreak trees at maturity. If there is a gap in the windbreak, the wind will be channeled through this opening as if it were a wind tunnel, and the wind speed can actually increase.

Windbreaks can be designed on a smaller scale for suburban homes. The key is to create a barrier of plants that runs perpendicular to the direction of the prevailing winds or those that most commonly blow during winter storms. Windbreaks are usually composed of evergreen trees and shrubs, because deciduous plants have no leafy barrier during the winter when protection is needed most.

PLANT A TREE OR SHRUBS TO BLOCK COLD WINDS.

If you live on a small lot and would like to reduce cold winds, a single well-placed evergreen tree or large shrub can have a big effect. Determine which direction the wind comes from during winter and locate your tree on the windward side of the house. Although it will cast a shadow, hardy evergreens are still the most effective trees for this purpose. You can increase your home's wind protection by adding dense foundation planting around the base of the outer building walls.

PLANT A MINIATURE WINDBREAK ALONG THE EDGE OF YOUR LOT.

Windbreaks not only reduce the direct exposure of your house to cold wind, they can also make outdoor living spaces more comfortable in winter. If the windbreak is located along a fence line, a solid board fence or wall will effectively block wind on a lower level. This eliminates the need for trees that branch low to the ground or the addition of shrubs to close gaps between trunks. Trees chosen for this pur-

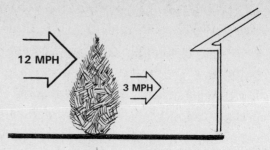

EVERGREEN WINDBREAK
Most single-row evergreen windbreaks are less than 70 percent dense. Areas inside the windbreak will still experience a breeze, but it will be greatly reduced if the windbreak trees are planted close together.

pose must have sufficient canopy density higher up to block the wind, and they have the added benefit of screening views of neighboring homes.

Be aware of your neighbor's solar needs. If you plant a windbreak, it may eventually provide unwanted shade next door. Likewise, your neighbor's windbreak could shade your south side and destroy the benefits of solar-friendly landscaping. If you or your neighbor has solar panels on the roof, be doubly aware of how your trees can reduce or even eliminate the sunlight required to make them function properly.

A brick wall is 100 percent dense and allows no wind to pass through it. A single windrow of tightly spaced evergreen trees creates a windbreak that is less effective. Few windrows are more than 70 percent dense, which means 30 percent of the wind still passes through. Based on the maximum benefit of 70 percent density, this barrier will reduce air speeds on the lee side from 60 to 75 percent. This can save up to 10 percent on your winter heating bill.

SHELTERBELTS

As far back as 1789, Mennonite farmers from Germany immigrated to the Russian steppes and there began to plant large windbreaks several rows thick around their fields to thwart the merciless wind. Today there are thousands of miles of these ancient dense windbreaks protecting millions of acres of Russian farmland.

European immigrants who settled the American Great Plains brought with them their knowledge of these beefed-up windbreaks, which combined evergreen and deciduous trees with shrubs to create a wider and denser barrier than a single windrow. From the start they planted seedlings in the virgin land, which would one day grow large enough to reduce wind erosion, protect homes, and encourage winter crop production. These arrangements, called "shelterbelts," are most successful in protecting homesites on the Midwestern prairie, where the icy winds are persistent. They are also effective in coastal communities, which must contend with brutal onshore breezes. A traditional single-row or even double-row windbreak would not be nearly as effective under these extreme conditions.

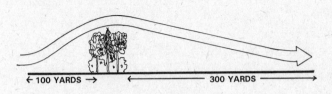

← 100 YARDS →   ← 300 YARDS →

SHELTERBELT
Wind speed is slowed for 100 yards on the windward side of a 30-foot-tall shelterbelt. It also slows wind up to 300 yards downwind from the shelterbelt. This illustrates how a mature shelterbelt can cause profound changes in air movement over very large areas.

Shelterbelts encounter wind on the outside or windward side, while the lee side remains relatively calm. The speed of the wind entering the shelterbelt is slowed as it bounces around inside, and by the time it's ready to exit the lee side there is very little energy left. A well-planned space between the shelterbelt and a house becomes less turbulent and more like dead air, a buffer that keeps much of the raw cold wind from making direct contact with the house. Shelterbelts are also very effective in controlling snow drift. The lee edge of a shelterbelt should be located 20 to 60 feet from the building wall. You can also plant a second insulating barrier of evergreens up against the house, as described above, to create a dead-air space immediately around the foundation walls.

Locating and sizing shelterbelts for a larger piece of property should be carefully thought out. Factors such as wind speed, local land forms, and snow drift must all be taken into consideration. For free advice on larger properties, contact the nearest office of the USDA Soil Conservation Service, a federal agency charged with the preservation of agricultural land. You can also discuss the project with state or county agricultural offices, farm advisers, or university extension agents who are knowledgeable about local conditions.

SPECIES FOR WINDBREAKS AND SHELTERBELTS

Botanical Name	Common Name	Height (in feet)	Spacing (in feet)
Acer **spp**	Maples	25–90	4
†Acer ginnala	Amur maple	20	4
†Acer negundo	Box elder	60	6
†Amelanchier alnifolia	Saskatoon	20	4
†Caragana arborescens	Siberian pea tree	18	4
Carpinus betulus	European hornbeam	60	4
Cornus mas	Carnelian cherry	24	4
Crataegus phaenopyrum	Washington hawthorne	30	4
†Eleagnus angustifolia	Russian olive	20	6
*Eucalyptus **spp**	Gum tree	100	6
Forsythia intermidia	Forsythia	9	4
†Fraxinus pennsylvanica	Green ash	60	6
*†Juniperus communis	Common juniper	3–30	2
Ligustrum amurense	Amur privet	15	2
*Ligustrum japonicum	Japanese privet	6–18	3
†Lonicera tatarica	Tatarian honeysuckle	9	3
†Maclura pomifera	Osage orange	60	6
Philadelphus coronaris	Sweet mockorange	9	3
*Picea abies	Norway spruce	100	6
†*Picea glauca	White spruce	90	6
†*Picea pungens	Colorado blue spruce	100	6
†*Pinus banksiana	Jack pine	75	4
*Pinus nigra	Austrian pine	90	6
*Pinus strobus	White pine	100	6
†*Pinus sylvestris	Scotch pine	70	6
†Populus **spp**	Poplar, cottonwood	50–100	4
†Prunus virginiana	Chokecherry	30	4
Quercus imbricaria	Shingle oak	75	12
†Quercus macrocarpa	Burr oak	75	12
Rhamnus frangula columnaris	Tall hedge buckthorn	12	2
†Salix alba	White willow	75	6
†Shepherdia argentea	Buffalo berry	18	3
Syringa amurensis	Japanese lilac	30	4
Tilia cordata "Greenspire"	Greenspire linden	40	4
†Ulmus pumila	Dwarf elm	75	6
Viburnum prunifolium	Blackhaw	15	3
Viburnum sieboldi	Siebold viburnum	30	4

* Indicates evergreen.
† Indicates rugged and hardy species suitable for the Great Plains shelterbelts.
spp Indicates many species of this genus are suitable.

Most shelterbelts consist of very hardy, strong-branching, wind-resistant trees, although some flowering specimens can be spotted in for interest and visual quality. The anatomy of a typical shelterbelt consists of three staggered rows, but more can be added, if desired, to make it less rigid in form. The smaller shrubs on the outer windward side of the shelterbelt help deflect wind upward so that some of its energy goes over the top of the barrier rather than through it.

Row 1 Tall, fast-growing deciduous trees on lee side

Row 2 Evergreen trees—usually conifers—in the middle

Row 3 Combination of shrubs and small trees on the outside

Trees and shrubs typically used in shelterbelts are planted in small sizes so they will root and become well anchored in the soil. Since they must sustain very heavy wind loads in their early years, they require sufficient rooting to stand up to the strain. Trees with root balls the shape of a nursery container take more time to develop a strong rooting network or taproot. Some never do root well.

The ideal small-sized tree is easily obtained in quantity from tree farms, which grow huge quantities of seedlings for farmers and reforestation projects. Most growers will send you a catalog or availability list if you call or write with your request. You'll be very surprised how inexpensive the plants are when field-grown in huge quantities, particularly when they are shipped directly to your home. In fact, they even sell their *evergreens* bare root, which eliminates the extra cost of a pot or burlap and facilitates shipping.

To plant very large windbreaks and shelterbelts, rent a trenching machine so you won't have to dig individual holes. Actual spacings between rows and individual trees or shrubs will vary, so it's best to consult an experienced Soil Conservation Service agent or another professional familiar with local conditions before you buy plants or begin digging.

CHAPTER 7

RECYCLING WASTE FROM HOUSE AND GARDEN

Budget gardening is a mindset. The key is to shift from the consumer mentality to that of the hunter-gatherer. In countries where people live off the land, a tremendous amount of thought and creativity goes into how best to use each resource at hand. There are no junk cars or discarded appliances, because the people value the tempered steel for spear points and sheet metal for roofs, and turn the rest of the vehicle over to dozens of other day-to-day uses. Yet here in the United States we can't even *give* away an old car, for they are too commonplace and serve only to be crushed in the wrecking yard for scrap iron.

Perhaps our downfall is our lust for convenience. It's easier to eat off disposable paper plates than to wash dishes after each meal, but we must buy those paper plates, and of course that means spending money. Thus we weigh the cost of disposables against the effort required to recycle or reuse. But in fact there are myriad ways we can reuse obvious and not-so-obvious items in the garden.

WOOD

Sticks—Never Throw Them Out Again

I can always tell when it's garbage pickup day in a neighborhood, because beautifully trimmed bundles of whips and twigs, the waste from someone's pruning efforts, are set out on the curb. Every stick is cut to the same length, leafless and begging to be reused, yet inevitably they end up in the landfill. So much work to create so much waste!

Yet there are numerous examples from around the globe of people who have discovered uses for this "waste" and in turn teach us about the true art of horticulture. A Zulu cattleman who, even if it were available, could never afford enclosures of milled lumber, fashions picket fences of twigs and branches, all irregular but beautiful. A cottage gardener from the British countryside weaves the still-green suckers and water sprouts from his fruit trees into a wattle fence so it resembles a well-made basket. An old Italian outside Rome cuts his stone pines when they threaten to fall over, and uses the branches for a rustic garden bench in the shade of his beloved cypress. What all these people have in common is their ability to transform scrap wood from their gardens into attractive and useful amenities.

Whenever you prune, or when you have a tree or shrub removed from a landscape, you will be left with some waste material. Long whiplike growths, usually suckers around the base of tree trunks and water sprouts, are some of the most useful. These grow quickly, are very straight and evenly tapered, and usually lack side branches. You'll have to make some extra cuts in order to harvest these sticks into usable twigs, but it pays off in the long run. Examine each newly removed branch and remove any unnecessary growth and leaves.

If you don't have any material of this sort in your own yard, a "garbage day" harvest may provide it. Simply drive around either the night before garbage day or very early in the morning until you find the right-sized bundle out on the curb. This is a perfect way to obtain all sorts of twigs that patient folks (usually frugal senior citizens) have already cleaned up for you. The best time to find these is winter, when gardeners are dormant-season pruning.

Other sources of similar and plentiful materials are orchard farmers in and around urban areas, because they must do extensive pruning each year. They usually burn this excess material, but they might let you pick through their piles beforehand. Big tree-trimming companies, which usually chip their prunings, are not the best source, but small pruning services or residential gardeners don't usually have the equipment to chip their prunings and must cart them off to the dump. Call up and express your desire to obtain sticks. You might also check with the local landfill, because during pruning season they are no doubt deluged with the stuff.

COPPICING—ENDLESS SUPPLY OF STICKS

On early American homesteads there was always a demand for flexible materials to bind split-rail fences and for straight twigs to make frontier picket fences. Long strands of weeping willow were favored for split-rail bindings, because they were easy to wrap when green, and when they dried out in this contorted shape, they bound the fence securely.

Poplar and willow are two of the fastest-growing trees, and their tendency to produce quality suckers in quantity made them an important resource. A farmer would start a few of these trees on his land if there were no wild plants available. Each winter the plants would be cut back severely to the stumps, stimulating vigorous suckering during the following growing season. Every other year or so when the trees were bare, the farmer would prune off the suckers to be used right away while green or stored for future use.

Coppicing is a good way for budget gardeners to put in a crop of quality sticks every year or so. But since poplar and willow are so vigorous and invasively rooted, and because coppicing does not render them particularly attractive, this method is recommended only for larger homesites, where the coppicing plants may be hidden from view. Many Native American tribes practiced coppicing of wild plants to encourage production of certain types of growth suited to basketmaking.

On a larger scale, this concept is used to produce poles in countries where timber is scarce. Plantations in drier climates cannot support the water-hungry poplar or willow, so the trees used are the highly drought-tolerant eucalyptus and acacia, which sprout readily from stumps. They are planted in closely spaced rows like an orchard, and after the first harvest the stumps are allowed to sucker. Fire and pruning are used to eliminate any lateral growth in order to produce the longest, most evenly tapered poles possible. Anyone who lives on a large homesite, with the space to produce such poles, will find they have dozens of uses, from fence posts to roof joists, which cost no more than the price of gas to fuel the chain saw.

Twisted sticks are often used in flower arrangements or in contemporary decor, where they are appreciated for their naturally exotic shapes. The best way to obtain these free of charge is by growing a corkscrew willow, *Salix matsudana 'Tortuosa.'* This tree grows as easily from unrooted cuttings as the rest of the willow clan and makes a fine landscape tree. After pruning or thinning in the winter, when it's bare, you can take your pick of the twisted sticks, which will range from 6 inches to 16 feet or more in length. To prevent the buds from sprouting leaves in the sudden warmth of your home, lay them out on a flat surface to dry before you use them indoors.

BAMBOO AND CANES

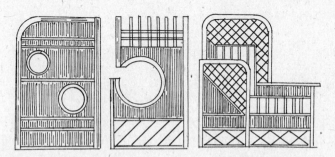

JAPANESE BAMBOO FENCES
The Japanese have made bamboo fence building an art. They lash the canes together into all sorts of shapes and patterns.

It is well known that bamboo and its close relatives are awesomely invasive in cultivated gardens. Fast-growing and aggressive once established, they can be sheer hell to remove, yet from this clan much of Asia obtains its building materials. Bamboo is a gold mine for budget gardeners, because cane is one of the strongest and most attractive sticks. Technically a grass, it has very rigid fibers, with each segment an independent empty cylinder. Canes have no lateral branching to disturb the straight, gradually tapering forms and are also quite resistant to decomposition.

Before you get too excited, think twice before planting bamboo for your own private supply of canes. It's better to find an abandoned stand or one unwanted in some other poor soul's garden. You can go in and make a single cutting to store many years' supply for future use. In the Deep South and other mild climates, bamboo is easy to find, as it has adapted perfectly to the warm winters and totally engulfs many unfortunate homes.

If you're lucky enough to find a good stand of timber bamboo, you'll discover it is truly monumental in proportion with canes up to 30 feet long and 4 inches in diameter. Bring a hand ax or saw and long-handled loppers, because you can't cut this stuff easily with clippers. If you plan to keep very long canes intact, be sure your vehicle is able to transport them safely, and keep a red flag on hand to tie at the end.

Another alternative is a common relative of bamboo, giant reed cane, *Arundo dondax*. It is more tolerant of cold and drought than most bamboo and was favored in the nineteenth century for fishing poles. It manages to persist at some homesteads, and where there is sufficient water it has become a tenacious weed. Still, giant reed is a good choice for cane supply, but plant it with some sort of barrier, such as sheet metal, surrounding the root ball to control its tendency to spread.

STICK PREPARATION AND STORAGE

It is important to know how to prepare your sticks for use. Experts who make bent-willow furniture cut their willow only in the early spring, when sap begins to flow and the buds swell. But for most other uses you can cut year-round, and if the material must bend or be flexible enough to weave, it should be used immediately. You can soak stored twigs in water or wrap them in wet carpet to retain moisture flexibility for a longer period, as willow furniture-makers do. Otherwise, every day after the twig is cut it becomes drier and stiffer. If the twigs are to be used as stakes or supports of any kind, they should be allowed to dry on a clean, flat surface. A concrete slab or gravel is fine. If they sag or bend even slightly, the dried twig will always retain that shape. In moist climates, the sticks should be dried in the sun to avoid rotting as they harden off. You can set them out on the roof, where they will be well above the ground and receive full sun exposure.

Topiary forms are all the rage today, and the garden catalogs are filled with ready-made bent-wire frames upon which to grow evergreen vines such as creeping fig and dwarf ivy. You can create your own frames using your gathered sticks. While the sticks are still soft, insert them into decorative flowerpots and tie them into tepees, arches, hearts, grids, or other shapes. Plant the pot with evergreen vines or a fast-growing annual, such as black-eyed-Susan. Frameworks of sticks lashed together are much more attractive and rustic if the vine does not cover the entire shape and the sticks themselves become an integral part of the decorative effect.

STICK FENCING

When the pilgrims came to the New World they protected their gardens from live-stock and wildlife with paling fences. These rustic picket fences were made of twigs or split stakes pounded into the ground and connected by a single top rail. This type of fence appears worldwide, made of as many different kinds of wood as there are trees. Sometimes the stakes are connected with a sapling wired to the tops of the pickets; other times wire is woven in and around the twigs into long strips of flexible fence. This fence is easiest to build if you use sticks of similar diameters that have been dried flat until they are rigid enough to stand well. The top need not be even, as the irregular lengths add character.

Canes and bamboo also make excellent fencing. In Japan, the art of bamboo fencing and screens has yielded some beautiful yet functional works of art. The cane is drilled with small holes into which wire is threaded for secure fastenings. Those who have the skill and ability for such intricate projects should consult one of the many good books on Japanese gardens to find some examples of bamboo art to copy. Otherwise, canes can be used much the same way as pickets and are lovely additions to tropical and Asian-inspired gardens.

Originally wattle fences enclosed sheep pastures or kitchen gardens where their density, greater than that of paling fences, made them stronger and more restrictive to small animals. This density also helped thwart the biting cold winds common in the British Isles.

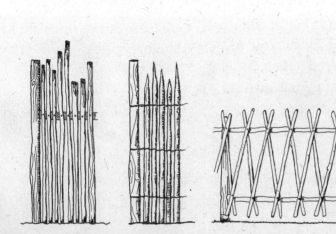

STICK FENCES
LEFT: *This is similar to the first picket fences of Plymouth Colony. Split stakes were pounded into the soil and the tops connected by a stringer.* CENTER: *Another adaptation of the picket fence uses intact sticks that have been sharpened to a point. The sticks are then woven together with twisted wire stringers.* RIGHT: *This is just one of many adaptations of sticks into rigid decorative fences.*

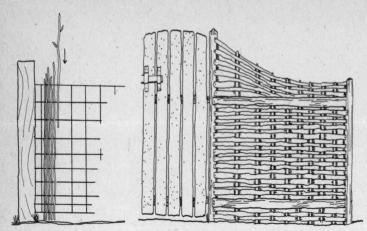

WATTLE FENCING
Shown here are two different ways to create the wattle effect of Old World fencing. LEFT: *This is a simplified version of true wattle. It is basically a wire field fence with green cuttings woven in and out of the wire grid. When they dry and harden off, the sticks become very rigid.* RIGHT: *Nothing compares with the charm of true wattle fencing, but it is very labor-intensive. The difficulty is anchoring the vertical stays so they hold up while you weave in the wattle.*

Wattle utilizes a series of vertical stays or tightly spaced posts secured in the soil. Green wood whips are then woven horizontally in and out of these posts until they produce a basket-like wall that can be made completely opaque. Once the woven wood dries, the fence hardens and becomes very durable and stable. Building a wattle fence from scratch is a difficult task but will yield a unique and very beautiful barrier.

A similar effect can be achieved with far less effort where woven wire fencing is already in place. This mesh becomes a framework through which you can weave fresh green whips. The wire fencing should have large openings, because the whips cannot take sharp bends without breaking. The whips can be woven from top to bottom or horizontally, which is simpler to do with field fencing that has rectangular openings. It may help to tie the ends of each stick securely with baling wire to keep them from popping out of place as the wood dries. The size of the whips and their density can be varied according to what you have on hand and the degree of transparency desired. It takes a lot of material to create a wattle fence, so don't be surprised if it becomes a long-term project following each year's winter pruning.

GARDEN USES FOR STICKS

There is an endless number of uses for twigs in the garden, and anyone with an empty wallet or creative flair will find them indispensable. Once you have a good supply of straight twigs on hand, you'll discover new ways to employ them in your garden. For example, the thorny twigs of roses and berry vines can be carefully arranged in planters to keep cats and dogs from spoiling the flowers.

PLANT AND FLOWER STAKES

Straight twigs make beautiful flower stakes. Rather than artificial-appearing metal or bamboo, twigs are naturally colored and irregular enough to be quite charming. Stakes come in handy in the kitchen garden as well, to support leaning plants, define planting areas, and mark where underground roots or bulbs are located. Be sure to trim and dry the stakes before using them so they will be stiff enough to push the end into damp soil without bending.

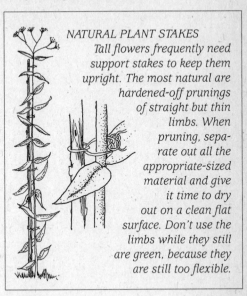

NATURAL PLANT STAKES
Tall flowers frequently need support stakes to keep them upright. The most natural are hardened-off prunings of straight but thin limbs. When pruning, separate out all the appropriate-sized material and give it time to dry out on a clean flat surface. Don't use the limbs while they still are green, because they are still too flexible.

TEPEE

Take a peek into any early-American kitchen garden and you'll find pole tepees cloaked in pole-bean vines. Simple to make by binding the ends of sticks together with bailing wire, they may be used year after year for beans, peas, gourds, and other vine plants. Don't disassemble the tepee at the end of the season; simply pull it out of the ground, gather the poles together like the spokes of an umbrella, and set it aside for the next year.

TEPEE TRELLIS
Long, straight limbs are ideal for creating climbing bean supports, a method that was practiced by the first America colonists.
LEFT: *This is the traditional tepee, which may have many more poles than the three shown here.*
RIGHT: *A wider A-frame design allows you to attach wire or netting for more dainty climbing plants such as peas, which may not be capable of attaching themselves to the larger-diameter poles.*

PEA TRELLIS

Peas climb by slender tendrils, which wrap more easily around thin objects than thicker ones. That's why garden centers sell special netting for both edible peas and flowering sweet peas. Rather than spend the money on such a trellis for climbing peas, save some of your thinnest twiggy branches from winter pruning. First, string a horizontal wire between posts where the peas are to grow. Then take the branches, turn them upside down, and hang them in this position on the wire so the twig tips nearly touch the ground. These slender tips are ideal for young pea tendrils to grab hold, and are stronger farther up for when the vines mature and need better support.

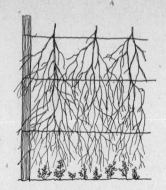

TWIGGY PEA TRELLIS
An old-style pea trellis is easy to make using some of your finer branching winter prunings. The twiggy branches are attached upside down to a wire stringer so that the finest twigs, at the tips, are within reach of developing pea vines.

WALL TRELLIS

Nothing is more charming than a wall trellis made of twigs and branches. Twigs with diameters averaging about $^3/_4$ inch or so can be lashed with wire or rawhide into attractive grids and arches. Attached to walls, fences, and doorways, these support climbing plants. Many garden-supply catalogs sell rustic trellises at astounding prices, but it doesn't make sense to buy one when they are as simple to build as a ladder and infinitely more charming than those milled, red-stained prefabricated fan or grid trellises.

There are different ways to attach these trellis twigs. Some people prefer to predrill holes

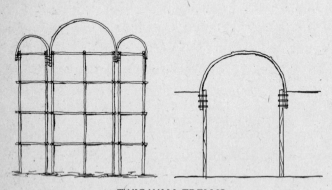

TWIG WALL TRELLIS
Why not try lashing or nailing together a trellis of twigs to support vines? They are particularly beautiful with annual morning-glory vines. To get more ideas for patterns, consult pricey garden-supply catalogs, which usually picture at least one easily copied design.

and make the connections with wood screws, then cover the screw heads with more attractive lashing material, such as twine, leather, or even thin, viny materials. Don't forget that any trellis design that requires bends or arches should use green flexible materials for the curved parts, so they dry in the proper shape.

STEP RISERS

In many gardens a steeply sloped pathway can become too difficult to use in wet weather. A simple solution is to create widely spaced steps to take up the grade more comfortably. These steps are usually created out of railroad ties placed across the pathway and anchored into place by reinforcing bar or steel pipe pounded into the ground. The area behind this step riser is filled with earth or brick.

If you have to cut some heavy limbs or fell a tree, the larger-diameter branches or logs can be employed as free step risers, particularly hardwood, cedar, or redwood, which resist decomposition. These logs are laid on the ground and anchored with metal stakes, just as with the railroad ties. To make safe steps, use lengths as wide as the path, and from 6 inches to 8 inches in diameter to equal the riser height dictated by building codes. You can also use logs of this diameter as rustic flowerbed edging.

GATEWAY ARCHES

Gateways become something special if they have overhead arches upon which vines or roses can be trained. Whether arched, pointed, or simply flat-topped, they transform sticks into stunning architectural features. When enveloped in flowering vines, they make especially inviting entries. When you consider what it costs to make a similar structure of milled lumber, you will realize that your efforts will be worthwhile.

There are many ways to create these arches, depending on the type of gate already in place. What all share is two strong, upright support poles that are attached to the existing gate posts with wood screws, nails, or tie wire. These will carry the weight of the vine and should be securely fastened.

You can add the arch or crosspiece by using screws or a secure lashing with wire. Exactly how they are placed depends on your design. Always remember that this little structure will take a beating, so when in doubt, choose the most long-

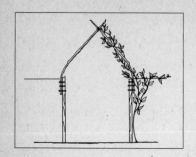 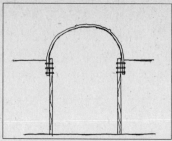 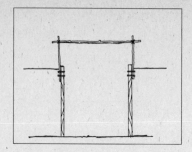

TWIG GATEWAY ARCH

You don't have to hire a carpenter to add those charming vine-shrouded gateways to your house. Simply use the fence posts already in place and attach some stout twigs with wood screws or nails. Then use one of these three design ideas to create an overhead connection. These are just a few of the many options you can try, and since they are made of unwanted twigs, there's no cost for experimenting.

lasting connections, such as long wood or drive screws. It helps to pre-drill the holes, since dried wood tends to be much less yielding than green wood.

SHADE ARBORS

Constructing an arbor is a bigger job, but a whole industry has grown up around the use of treated lodgepole pines as rustic arbors. Anything you cut or find for this use is valuable, since the alternative—milled lumber or lodgepole—can be exorbitantly priced and never projects the same appealing, rustic character of twig work. Some of the best sources of pole wood are acacia, alder, cedar, eucalyptus, maple, and poplar. They can be grown in dense, woodlot-type blocks for a single cutting, or coppiced on a larger scale as a renewable resource for poles. The creation of overhead structures is a job best left to those experienced in construction to ensure that the structure won't collapse and cause injury. Providing the materials, however, will save you a great deal in the overall cost.

FURNITURE

It's simple to create garden furniture out of branches, although making detailed twig furniture like that sold in catalogs is by no means a beginner project. There are many different methods for creating this type of furniture, from bent willow furniture to burl tables. There are numerous how-to books on this subject available for detailed instructions and creative inspiration. If you are an artistic person or enjoy crafts, give it a try.

WREATHS

Grapevine runners made ideal framework wreaths because they are long and flexible. A single grape plant, whether it fruits or not, is an unlimited source of core wreath material. But wreaths can be made out of virtually any kind of stick that can be curved into the circular shape. Imagine a wreath made of winter-cut willow whips, which bursts into leaf once brought indoors where it is warm. Whether you opt for a wreath that is purely decorative or combine unique gleanings such as culinary herbs, dried rose hips, pomegranates, and dried flowers, consider all your vine-plant prunings as a resource for wreath making.

To make a core wreath, you'll need a pair of needle-nose pliers and some tie wire. Use your materials when freshly cut, because once they dry out, much of their flexibility is lost. To begin, choose one very strong whip, make a circle the size of your finished wreath with a few inches of overlap at the ends. Securely bind the overlapped portion together with wire so it won't come apart. Then begin adding more whips by tying them to this core circle until your wreath is about the thickness and size you imagined. Then use a hot-glue gun or florist's wire to attach the decorations.

PLANTS THAT WILL PROVIDE YOU WITH SOME OF THE BEST CORE WREATH MATERIALS

Plant	Type
Birch	Tree
Bittersweet	Vine
Bridalwreath spiraea	Shrub
Dogwood	Tree
Grape	Vine
Honeysuckle	Vine
Kiwi	Vine
Redbud	Shrub/tree
Trumpet creeper	Vine
Willow	Tree
Wisteria	Vine

A ROCKY HARVEST

For those who must live with the difficulties of rocky soil, there are benefits as well. Rocks can range in size from pebbles to huge landscape boulders that require heavy moving equipment, but it's the middle sizes that are most valuable in garden making. One of the rules of budget gardening is to use the materials at hand before pursuing more complicated and expensive alternatives. If you have rocks, then use them!

When you build a raised planter or wall with stones, you'll never have to worry about its decomposition, as you do with wood. Stones encrusted with dirt can be cleaned up nicely by either rainfall or sprinklers, even after they are put to use. Working with stones isn't difficult, but it takes time to gather and transport your rocks to the location of your project. Then you must fit them together as tightly as possible in order to ensure stability. Use the larger stones on the bottom and the smaller stones farther up. For durable dry stone walls of any height, the base must be much wider than the top to achieve a strong barrier.

Rocks of any size are perfect to create a rock garden, one of the most interesting and charming natural-planting schemes. Rock gardens have long been a solution to very heavy soils or poor drainage in areas where these conditions are prevalent. The garden is created by placing large stones within the planting area, then filling in between them with soil. This raises the root zone above the difficult soils, ensuring rapid drainage. Rock gardens are also created on slopes where fewer rocks are needed and the soil is naturally shallow. The rocks creating this type of drainage are essential for those who enjoy plants such as succulents, which tend to rot if soils are too wet.

ROCK GARDENS AND PLANTERS
TOP: *Use those un-wanted rocks and boul-ders to create a rock garden. Arrange them in a creative pattern, then fill in the gaps with topsoil. Plant in the pockets, and soon nothing but the stones and flowering plants will be visible. This is ideal where soils are dense or so rocky that normal culti-vation is difficult.* BOTTOM: *Rocks can be stacked up to create raised planter walls. If sufficiently-sized pockets and gaps are allowed, then plants can spill down the wall as well as grow out of the top.*

The British are avid rock-garden enthusiasts, because of their love of alpine flowers. At the tops of mountains, above the tree line, small but beautiful plants thrive in the rocky, poor soil of the higher elevations. To create a suitable environment for alpines, gardeners must re-create these often arid, poor-fertility conditions using rocks and boulders.

The beauty of rock gardens is

that no two are alike. This is because the availability and type of stone vary with every region, and stone in general is not consistent in size and shape. Many believe the success of rock gardens is due to the fact that stones act as insulation and trap moisture beneath them, which keeps plant roots cool even when temperatures on the surface are very high. In hill country, it's not uncommon to see lush perennial wildflowers sprouting out of barren fractured stone cliffs, which is a natural example of this same moisture-holding capacity.

It's simple even for beginner gardeners to create their own rock garden, but it is essential to have plenty of stone on hand, since much of it will be buried. It's best to begin with the largest rocks and arrange them evenly over the area as a framework. Then use medium-sized and small rocks to fill in the spaces. Only after these are all set do you add the soil, which should contain plenty of sand to encourage fast drainage. Pockets of soil created between rocks are where you plant, and eventually the whole garden will come together, as the succulents, alpines, annuals, and perennials fill in and nestle among the stones.

Here are some other uses for rocks and stones:

ROCK MULCH

A free way to control weeds, rock mulch reduces soil-moisture loss and protects plant roots from heat or cold. These stones can be slightly larger or smaller than the size of your fist and should be laid out directly onto garden soil in a tightly packed single layer. Some weeds will pop through, but not many. The famous British gardener Vita Sackville-West was quite outspoken about rocks in her gardening columns. She was convinced that perennials that grew beside or among rocks were more productive, because their roots were cooler, and since the rocks prevented surface evaporation from the soil, the source of moisture was more consistent.

COBBLE PAVING

This is a great way to make quaint garden paths and small patios that blend perfectly into natural surroundings and need not be impeccable to keep down the mud and weeds. Either dig out the entire area to the depth of your stones, or dig out a tiny spot for each stone as you go. Set the stones so the tops are roughly at the same level, but keep in mind that this is a crude method, and over time with freeze-thaw or traffic, the paving can become very irregular. Once the stones are in place, pour dry masonry mortar mix over the top and brush it into all the crevices. Saturate the mortar with a fine mist from the garden hose, then allow a day or two for the whole thing to set. Although this surface is not suitable for high heels, it is definitely the most charming way to make a cheap or free path.

PLANTER EDGING

Planter edging can also be made from rocks. If the planter borders a lawn, it's a good idea to dig a shallow trench and set the rocks in low, because it's difficult to get the mower close enough to a taller stone. Where planters border patios or walkways, the stones can be larger.

HOUSEHOLD DISPOSABLES

Once you start viewing your household refuse in budget-gardening terms, you'll be amazed how much can be reused in the garden. Although manufacturers are trying to conserve on packaging, there are still many cases where the container costs nearly as much as the contents. Although we can't avoid many of these products, the ability to reuse them to the fullest extent helps mitigate the problem.

CONSIDER YOUR PLASTICS

Plastic is molded into containers of every shape and size. It does not rust, leak, become saturated, or provide food for any pests. Space-age blending has made today's plastics more durable than ever before. To take full advantage of disposable plastics, you'll need a simple hacksaw or strong scissors, because most of the time they must be altered, usually by cutting. You may also discover that the wall thicknesses of plastic containers vary. Thin walls are fine, but they won't hold up as long as thick ones and tend to be more difficult to handle after the container is cut.

As we saw in Chapter 5, many aspects of plant propagation require containers. Containers may be small and support one seedling or larger to start a gang of seedlings. Plastic is ideal, but the contents of household disposables often contain substances toxic to plants. For example, residue of liquid laundry detergent in the empty jug must be cleaned out before soil can be added. It's tough to wash out a jug with a single small hole thoroughly, so it's better to cut the jug with your hacksaw into an open-topped container and then wash it out.

Once the container is cut and washed, you'll have to make holes in the bottom for drainage. One way is to take a hammer and a large nail and set the container on a piece of wood. Simply pound the nail and it will pierce the plastic. Be sure the hole is of sufficient size so that after you remove the nail it doesn't become restricted again. You can also punch holes with a Phillips head screwdriver, which is a lot thicker than a nail. Perhaps the most effective method is to heat a long, straight piece of coat hanger over your stove burner. Once hot, the wire will glide effortlessly through the plastic. In most cases you'll have to make numerous, regularly spaced holes to ensure that the container drains adequately.

Chances are you'll find yourself with lots of leftover container-top halves.

The handles of thicker containers can be cut into handy scoops for granular fertilizer or potting soil or implemented as funnels for pouring gasoline into your lawn mower.

EXAMPLES OF COMMON HOUSEHOLD PRODUCTS THAT ARE PACKAGED IN STRONG PLASTIC BOTTLES

Ammonia	Liquid drain cleaner
Antifreeze	Liquor—1.75 Liters
Bleach	Lotion
Cleaning products	Milk
Dishwashing soap	Syrup
Liquid detergent	

DISPOSABLE CONTAINERS
You can use virtually any plastic container for a planting pot. These four examples include containers for antifreeze, motor oil, soda, and liquid laundry detergent. Use scissors to cut the thinner materials and a hacksaw for thick plastic. After cutting, you may be left with the handle, which is easily cut into a handy scoop or a funnel.

When you are using recycled containers to grow plants, it's rare to find all in the same size and shape. To make them more manageable, you can place them in a flat, about 18 inches square, which is the tray that nurseries use to hold seedling bedding plants. If you can't obtain free surplus flats from your local plant seller, it's worth spending a little to buy a few or some handy alternatives that you'll be able to use over and over. Shallow plastic organizer trays and Tupperware-type storage boxes can be purchased cheaply at discount stores; other containers that work well are laundry baskets, clear under-the-bed storage boxes, crates, totes, and cubes. You may also find some reusable planting containers for starting quantities of seeds, but for this purpose you must poke holes in the bottom for drainage.

CHEAP-SCAPES CHOICES: Look to the dairy case for some of the neatest containers for starting seedlings or nurturing cuttings. Waxed paper products, such as milk cartons, tend to break apart after a short time but make first-class one-time-use pots for starting seeds. By the time they start to deteriorate, it's time to plant the seedling out in the garden anyway. Single-serving yogurt cups are nearly identical in size to those plastic pots sold in six-packs at the nursery. Since these are somewhat fragile, poke your drainage holes with a hot coat hanger. Cottage cheese, sour cream, spreadable cream cheese, margarine, and many other products are sold in slightly larger plastic containers, which are ideal for potting plants germinated in the yogurt cups. Don't forget the drainage holes.

There are some unique uses for the gallon milk jugs found in practically every family refrigerator. Those with screw-on tops are particularly valuable. If you cut off only the very bottom, you have a miniature greenhouse for seedlings or cuttings. Placed over a young plant, it helps retain moisture, block wind, insulate from frost, protect from pests and pets, reduce sunburn, and give shelter from snow and rain. To allow more oxygen into the mini-greenhouse, take off the lid or poke some small holes in the upper portion with a hot coat hanger. For even more control, poke some larger holes and plug them with old wine-bottle corks or candle stubs. These can be removed one by one, as the seedling grows, to harden off the plant and help it gently to become adapted to conditions outside its protective bell.

Yet another handy use for milk jugs is as watering devices. If you have to go out of town or would like to liquid-fertilize a plant efficiently, this will do the trick: Take a clean milk jug *with a screw-on cap*. Poke a very small hole in the bottom of the edge with a needle. Fill the jug with water or a fertilizer solution while you seal the outside of the hole with your fingertip. When it's full, screw down the cap tightly. While the cap is closed there is a vacuum, so nothing will drain out of the hole. But loosening the cap allows air in to break the vacuum. Place a full jug with the hole next to the stem of your plant and loosen the cap. You can adjust the rate of flow out the hole by turning the cap. This method is particularly valuable in dense clay soils or on slopes where water or a water-fertilizer mixture tends to run off before it can be absorbed.

Keep a few fully intact gallon jugs on hand. Next time you mix up liquid fertilizer or some of the recipes in this book, you can count on the jug holding exactly a gallon. Plus, leftover potion will store in plastic jugs on the shelf indefinitely.

We throw away far more plastic than containers and packaging. Plastic tablecloths and shower curtains make good weatherproof tarps for covering outdoor furniture or equipment. They can be used to gather and carry large piles of leaves to the compost pile. Even old plastic hard-shelled luggage can be recycled—after the hinges or latches are broken—into durable flats to grow plants from seed, or for patio, deck, or balcony herb and flower gardens. Be sure to poke some holes for drainage with a heated knife or coat hanger.

The next time you replace your plastic laundry basket, don't throw the old one out. If it's broken or torn, you can repair it easily with duct tape. Then line the basket with a heavy-duty plastic garden waste bag and poke a few holes in the bottom of the bag and the laundry basket. Fill it with potting soil or dirt and you'll get at least one season's worth of leaf or root crops.

Don't forget all those Styrofoam products that usually land in the trash. Fast-food containers hold up longer than you think. Coffee cups are nice and deep for seedlings or rooting cuttings. They can be discarded after a single use and are easy to strip off when you transplant root-sensitive seedlings.

CHEAP-SCAPES CHOICES: It pays to save the wire twist ties from products bagged in plastic. Those consisting of a wire core inside a paper ribbon are durable enough to tie your vines and other plants to their support structure. Plastic garbage bags are always packed with extra ties, either the plastic type or larger versions of wire twist ties. Rather than throw them away or allow them to accumulate in the kitchen drawer, keep the extras with your gardening supplies so they're always handy.

METAL PRODUCTS

Caution: Newly cut metal edges can be very sharp. Wear gloves whenever you are working with cans or cutting them for new uses.

Throughout Latin America you can find extensive patio and balcony gardens of plants potted in old tins, coffee cans, and other metal containers. Sure, they don't look so great after rust sets in, but this doesn't stop the Mexican gardener. We too can take advantage of every can that comes out of the kitchen. Most of the time we don't pay much attention to the size of containers at the store except when comparing prices. But supermarket sales or special purchases at discount outlets sometimes advertise handy 8-ounce cans of tomato sauce, and since most people need a 16-ounce or 32-ounce size for making spaghetti, they don't buy the smaller size. Budget gardeners, on the other hand, may find this small container perfect for starting seedlings, which adds a bonus to the already low sale price.

There are other uses for by-products of the canned-food industry. A 32-ounce can with the top and bottom cut out yields a clean, smooth cylinder, a perfect barrier for seedlings devastated by crawling pests such as cutworms. After planting, simply set the cylinder over the top of the seedling and press it firmly into the soil. Anything that might feed upon the tender new leaves will have to crawl up and over to reach the plant. The smooth surface of metal is difficult for some to scale, so the seedlings are temporarily protected.

You can double the effect by brushing a ring of sticky molasses around the outside of the can so that any pest able to crawl over gets bogged down in the sticky stuff. Cans also help reduce cold or hot wind damage to seedlings. If you put some clear plastic food wrap over the top and anchor it with a rubber band, you create a small, temporary greenhouse to retain moisture and heat during a cold snap. To remove the cylinder after the plant matures, simply cut it off with tin snips.

Cans also work well to protect the trunks of trees and shrubs from bark damage by string trimmers. If you can't drop the cylinder over the top of the plant, cut one side, spread the can apart, and slide it around the trunk, being careful not to nick the bark on sharp metal edges. The can should automatically come together again, but if it doesn't, you can secure it with duct tape. You can paint the cans to match the trunk of the plant or just let them rust naturally.

CHEAP-SCAPES CHOICES: If you run out of your own discarded containers, contact the nearest school. The cafeteria may have lots of containers about to be thrown out. Huge, heavy-duty plastic jugs for cooking oil are a precious and durable commodity. Restaurant-size cans serve many uses and are good for holding rooting cuttings, because they are large and deep. Gallon plastic or glass jars with screw-top lids are equally versatile both at home and in the garden.

The tops and bottoms of the cans are also useful, particularly those used to seal frozen juices, as these need not be cut at all and don't have ragged edges. Punch them with a nail and thread on a string, then hang the shiny reflective disks in fruit trees to frighten away birds. To retain the shiny finish and discourage rust, dip them in a liquid plastic sealer.

If you have trouble with ants climbing on patio furniture and outdoor tables, a classic remedy using cans can solve the problem. Simply place each leg of a table into an empty can with an inch of water in the bottom. If you're concerned about rust staining your paving, use the bottoms of half-gallon plastic milk jugs.

Never again throw out those neat little spice containers and jars. They serve dozens of uses, such as dusting plants for insect pests or storage and shaking out fine seed.

Some cans, such as those used for soda pop, are made of aluminum, a metal that is lightweight and resistant to rust. Certainly these would also make good containers, but it is better to recycle them because aluminum is so valuable and can be crushed into compact units. Cutting the tops off can be difficult, anyway.

BALING WIRE

If you use straw for your garden or buy hay, it comes in bales bound by two or three strands of baling wire. Never throw out this wire; there are dozens of uses for it. To avoid scrapes, entanglements, and accidents, store loose baling wire in neat bundles. Here are just a few of the numerous ways to reuse baling wire that would otherwise be discarded:

1. Thread a strand through segments of old garden hose for staking trees.
2. Stretch the wire between poles for a pea-vine trellis.
3. Wrap it tightly around the tops of stick-pole tepees for beans or tomatoes.
4. Use it to bind the sections of stick arbors over gateways.
5. Weave it in and out of picket sticks to bind segments of rustic fencing.
6. Securely bind sticks for a decorative wall trellis.

DRYING RACKS

Anyone who grows herbs or flowers to dry for decoration or crafts knows it's tough to find enough places to hang the bundles. It's not always possible to use nails if

PIERCED TIN FOR GARDEN LIGHTING

Five-pound coffee cans and large restaurant-sized cans can be easily turned into beautiful pierced-tin garden lighting. Pierced tin was widely used in antique pie safes, because it allowed air flow into these cabinets while excluding pests, and the sheets of tin were punched with holes in attractive designs such as stars or geometric patterns. This method can be used on tin cans to allow light from a candle or bulb to pass through. These metal luminarias can be placed around the garden at night when you are entertaining. Don't feel limited to big cans—little 16-ounce cans can hold a votive candle.

The challenge is punching a curved surface without misshaping or denting it. It's really quite simple, but to start you'll need an empty can about the size of a 5-pound coffee can. Cans that aren't painted but have paper labels that can be removed yield the most attractive results. Remove only the top lid.

1. Make a sturdy paper template as wide as the depth of the can and as long as its circumference. Brown shopping bags are ideal. It should wrap around the outside like a label.

2. Fill the can with water and place it in the freezer.

3. Lay out your design on the paper template, noting where each little hole should be punched. It's a good idea to use a ruler or compass to make the patterns as accurate as possible.

4. When the water in the can is solid ice, remove the can from the freezer and immediately tape the template to the outside like a label.

5. Use a hammer and a sharp nail or small Phillips-head screwdriver to punch holes where they are indicated on your design.

6. After all the holes are punched, remove the paper and allow the ice to melt. Pour out the water. If you are hanging the light fixture, turn it bottom-up, cut a hole where the cord would pass through the center and attach a socket. For candles, leave the lid intact. Allow the can to rust naturally or paint it with metal paint or sealer to reduce the rusting.

your ceiling is too high or you don't want a bunch of nail holes in your rafters or beams. The answer: racks from discarded refrigerators or ovens. With these, you need only hang the rack itself at a convenient height and you can tie all the bun-

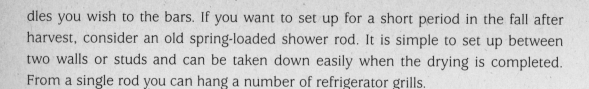

dles you wish to the bars. If you want to set up for a short period in the fall after harvest, consider an old spring-loaded shower rod. It is simple to set up between two walls or studs and can be taken down easily when the drying is completed. From a single rod you can hang a number of refrigerator grills.

BOOT SCRAPER

During the winter, boot scrapers are valuable, particularly in dense clay soils that stick tenaciously to the bottom of workboots. We tend to have a single scraper by the back door, but boots get heavy out in the garden, too. Mud mars wood decking, stains concrete walks, and leaves clods of dirt everywhere. It's easy to slip and fall with mud-coated boots. The budget gardening solution is to make your own boot scrapers out of old bottle caps and place them at strategic points throughout the garden. Take a heavy block of wood, or better yet, cut a round off a stump or firewood. Nail the bottle caps top down in tightly spaced rows until the entire surface is covered. Anchor the scraper by drilling two holes and pounding steel reinforcing bars through to fix it in the ground. The sharp, corrugated edges of bottle caps have been used for nearly a hundred years as boot scrapers and as curry combs for farm horses.

PAPER PRODUCTS

Every time you reuse or recycle a paper product, you are saving trees. Many paper-based products are disguised by wax or paint, yet these additives make them better suited for use in the garden. In classrooms across America, teachers use milk cartons to grow plants for science projects. Imagine how many single-serving milk and juice cartons are thrown out at schools and you have an idea of the enormous amount of reusable material that is available. They are simple to cut with a pair of scissors into containers of varying depths. The chief enemy to the longevity of these containers as pots for plants is the drain hole. Punching a hole punctures the wax sealer and introduces moisture into the paper core, which acts like a sponge. The cartons fare better if set upon a layer of gravel, which keeps the bottoms out of the wet, but the life span is still limited to a single season.

Round waxed-paper cartons used for ice cream also make good containers, and they have a snug-fitting lid. It's important to wash them out as soon as you empty the container and place it in the sun or somewhere else where it will dry out quickly.

Newspaper has dozens of uses in the garden. Newspaper ink is not toxic today as it once was. Of course, shredded newspaper used for packing material is a good mulch and breaks down far more quickly than sheet newsprint. If you find a working paper shredder at a garage sale, grab it. You'll be able to render your newspapers into first-rate mulch, even though it isn't too attractive.

Whole sheets also make a good weed-blocking mulch. Place a stack of five sheets or so where you wish, and wet them down so they stay put. This comes in handy for weed control in vegetable gardens. You can also cut newspapers into collars for trees and shrubs to discourage weeds from popping up beneath their lower branches. They are effective around the base of low-branching evergreens in lawn areas where it's tough to get the mower. It's a good idea to avoid sheets with colored ink, just to stay on the safe side.

Glass

Glass is one of the strongest materials available to us either cheap or free. One innovative gardener I know built an entire floor for his garden shed out of glass bottles. He was an avid Jim Beam drinker and saved the half-gallon bottles, which are square on the bottom and made of thick glass. He used a glass cutter to cut 6 inches off the bottom of each bottle so that every one was the same size. He dug out the soil to 6 inches in depth where the floor was to be, then laid out a sand-and-dry-mortar leveling bed on the bottom. One by one, he set in place each cut bottle, bottom up, and because they were square he could achieve a perfect fit using a level. When that task was completed, he staked a wood edging of 2-by-6 redwood into a tight-fitting frame. Since the bottles sat edge to edge, the frame served to keep them tightly bound together. Then he spread dry mortar over the bottles, sweeping it into the small cracks, and misted the entire mass with the garden hose so the mortar set into a long-lasting, albeit slippery, pavement. This method can be used outdoors as well, but irregularities in the surface will develop as the sand and bottles settle with the changing seasons.

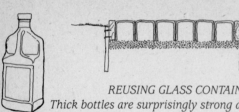

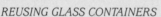
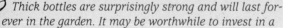

REUSING GLASS CONTAINERS
Thick bottles are surprisingly strong and will last for-ever in the garden. It may be worthwhile to invest in a glass cutter, or simply adapt these ideas using whole bottles. There is no limit to what you can do with bottle glass in the garden, so why not experiment? LEFT AND CENTER: *The thick half-gallon glass liquor bottles are very strong. You can cut off the bottoms to create unique paving or simply dig out the soil deeper and use the bottle intact. Dig out the area of the floor to the proper depth, then line it with sand as a leveling bed. Once the bottles are in place, add a frame of 2-by-4-foot or 2-by-6-foot redwood boards staked securely into place.* RIGHT: *You can create bed dividers or purely decorative accents in a garden using thick-bottomed wine bottles. Those of champagne are unusually thick and dark-colored, which reduces the glare and possibility of breakage. Either pound the bottles into soft soil, dig a trench and set them in, or dig small separate holes with a bulb planter or post-hole digger.*

An inventive mind can conjure up lots of other ideas for using bottles as paving. A post hole accommodates a half-gallon wine bottle inserted top down. In a shallower trench, thick-bottomed bottles, such as those for champagne, can be lined up as an edge for planters. When the sun hits them just right, you'll enjoy the unusual color. To get a quantity of these bottles, make the rounds of the local party bars after New Year's or contact places where wedding receptions are held. A really creative garden-art aficionado might cut the bottoms off colored bottles and combine them in a wet concrete slab with exotic glazed ceramic tile samples and smooth, rounded pebbles to create a beautiful and interesting paving accent.

In old Western ghost towns, such as Rhyolite, Nevada, you can find houses with entire walls made out of bottles. At one time the boomtowns were packed with saloons, which consumed thousands of bottles of whiskey and beer. Since timber and brick were scarce in the desert, the bottles were collected and stacked with mortar or cement into walls of incredible load-bearing strength. These walls did not often contain steel reinforcement, yet they could withstand heavy loads of snow, attesting to the compressive strength of glass. Strong winds, which generate horizontal pressure, led to the demise of many of these buildings.

There is no reason why we can't add glass bottles to our own garden creations. Those inspired enough to attempt building walls of adobe brick will find that bottles fit right in between the adobes. The same applies for spaces in mortared stone walls. The glass lends an interesting transparency, particularly if used on top, where more of the surface is exposed to sunlight.

WOOD

Whenever the kids enjoy Popsicles or ice cream with the little flat wooden sticks, make a point of collecting them before they go into the garbage can. They make good plant markers for seed flats or simply to identify plants in the garden, although they don't hold up as well as plastic. The advantage is that crayons are perfect for marking on wood, and in most households with children these are plentiful and free.

Thread spools were once made excusively of wood, but now they are often plastic. They can be used for hanging tools in the garage or garden shed. Simply slide a long nail through the center hole of the spool and nail it to the wall. Do the same for a second spool and place it beside the first, allowing 1 to 2 inches between them. This is strong enough to hold the lighter flat hand tools such as a leaf rake or broom.

ALL SORTS OF OTHER STUFF

MYLAR BALLOONS

Keeping birds away from fruit trees, berry vines, or other food crops can be a real problem, and casting a net over a full-sized tree is next to impossible. People have devised all sorts of ways to frighten birds by hanging stuff in the branches, like single-serving pie tins and long strips of black plastic, and sometimes the results resemble Christmas trees. Next time somebody gives you one of those shiny silver party balloons with messages printed on them, don't throw it away after all the helium leaks out. This lightweight, highly reflective material shimmers with the slightest breeze, resists decomposition, and holds up in all kinds of weather. Simply cut the balloon into ribbons about an inch wide and tie them to your trees.

CANDLE STUBS

If cork isn't handy, wax candle stubs make perfect plugs for holes in garden pots.

FELT HATS

The thick felt used to make hats is usually wool and a good insulation material. It can be cut to the shape of your foot and inserted into the knee-high rubber boots (Wellingtons) used during winter. You might wish to glue them in place.

NYLONS AND PANTYHOSE

The legs of pantyhose make soft, flexible material for tying trees to support stakes. Young trees become stronger more quickly if allowed to move around a bit while still attached to their stakes. Pantyhose allows this movement without causing abrasion wounds on the tree bark.

KITCHEN GREASE

One of the few kitchen by-products that should not be added to the compost pile is grease. Don't toss this out, because birds just love it during the winter months when other food sources are scarce. The easiest way to get kitchen grease to wild birds is to pack it into the nooks and crannies of opened pinecones. Some avid birders enrich the offering by mixing the grease with rolled oats or birdseed before packing it into the cone. Or you can roll the cone in seed after you've packed in the grease. You'll find beef tallow thicker and more waxlike than the fat of pork or poultry, which makes it easier to work with. For this reason you may want to keep beef fat separate and avoid mixing it with that of other animals. Hang the fat-filled cones from trees where you can see them from indoors and enjoy the winter show. It's an old-time winter practice to tie uncooked fat rinds to bird feeders or tree twigs, as birds eat this, too.

CHICKENS AND GOATS—BACKYARD PROCESSING PLANTS

Certain domestic animals, such as chickens and goats, work as an efficient compost pile to transform kitchen waste into usable manure. In fact, these animals will eat refuse not suited to composting, which doubles their value. The only problem is that some communities have codes that forbid keeping "livestock" as opposed to pets like dogs or cats.

Much of the ill feeling toward animals in urban environments was caused by people who go overboard with their backyard livestock. A neighbor who keeps an entire flock of chickens with accompanying manure smells and flies on the other side of your swimming-pool fence spoils your enjoyment of the outdoors. Even worse is the single rooster, which, contrary to popular belief, insists on crowing morning, noon, *and* night. These problems result in laws prohibiting such animals, or the renewed enforcement of an old law that has gone largely ignored.

LAYING HENS

A laying hen is actually very quiet and goes about her business without much fuss. She rarely crows but will cackle from time to time, and you can count on a "range-fed" egg most days until the hen is too old to lay or molts. Chickens eat virtually anything that comes their way except raw potatoes and orange peels. They immediately consume your kitchen scraps or garden leavings, then promptly turn them into valuable manure. Best of all, you can feed them your unwanted pests—potato bugs, termites, ant nests, caterpillars, aphid-encrusted leaves, and virtually any other rich source of insect protein from the garden.

Keeping the manure raked up and pens clean ensures that neighbors won't have a problem with odors. Use plenty of wood shavings or straw bedding, then add it directly to the compost pile for an organic nitrogen boost. Another advantage at the end of the growing season is releasing chickens into your vegetable garden to consume insects before they can winter over. Likewise, in spring the birds will graze on the early crop of weeds or grass shoots, reducing the amount of vegetation to be tilled in before it's time to plant.

Some people create a double fence around their vegetable plots and allow the chickens to roam free in the "moat." The chickens gobble up any undesirable pests before they can cross the moat and enter the garden. The only thing a chicken needs is an occasional supplement of oyster shell, which is available at any feed store. Some people feed the hen's eggshells back to their chickens to replace the calcium, but old-timers claim this encourages them to peck and eat their own eggs.

You can tell she's due for a calcium supplement when her eggshells become thin and are easily broken.

Anyone serious about raising chickens can find baby chicks at most farm-supply stores in the spring. You can buy any number of chicks you wish, but the choice of breeds may be limited and rarely includes exotics. Baby chicks can be "sexed" at birth to separate out the hens, which cost more. When you buy "straight-run" chicks, that means they have not been sexed and you won't know the mix until later on. Expect about a 50–50 mix.

Roosters are undesirable because: (1) they become very aggressive with age, (2) they crow day and night, (3) fertile eggs rot much sooner than infertile ones. The little extra that you must pay for a guaranteed female more than makes up for the price of feeding a rooster chick until he exhibits the comb and tail of a mature bird. You can also buy a "pullet" (an older but still immature female that will soon begin laying) at premium prices later in the season.

If you live in the country and can use a larger flock, order the well-illustrated Murray McMurray Hatchery catalog. It contains more than 125 varieties of chickens, ducks, and more exotic fowl for incredibly low prices. This is because you are sent day-old hatchling chicks *by U.S. mail* in spring, and you must raise them under a heat lamp or brooder. Instructions are enclosed. You'd be surprised at how well these chicks tolerate shipping. Mix and match varieties as you please, from large meat breeds to the small, rare, or unusual. As long as you're going to have just one or two hens, why not choose an exotic breed that's decorative as well as useful? However, you must order at least thirty birds at a time from Murray McMurray so they keep one another warm while in transit. That's why it's a good idea to go in with a group of friends so that each of you has just a few birds to raise. Thirty chickens is a very big flock. For a color catalog, send $2 to: Murray McMurray Hatchery, Webster City, Iowa 50595-0458.

If you live in the country, be sure to protect your birds from predators. A hawk can swoop down and grab a young chicken right before your eyes. Birds are also vulnerable at night while they are roosting. Contrary to popular belief, chickens can fly, and if their pen is open they'll go right over the fence. Keep them in an aviary-type enclosure or a coop that can be sealed up tight at dusk to keep out foxes and coyotes.

GOATS

Another potential backyard manure machine is the pygmy goat. Standard goats are more difficult to contain and tend to climb, but pygmies are more like dogs and can be trained to remain docile. Goats are omnivorous and will eat everything from tree prunings to Brussels sprout stalks, which chickens won't touch. Be sure to provide your goats with plenty of food, because if they get hungry they'll strip the bark off trees and shrubs. Before you realize it's happening, you may lose some valuable plants.

The pellet-shaped manure of goats is not as potent as that of chickens and can be worked directly into garden soil or added to the compost pile. Goats are also valuable for "grubbing" out brush, particularly where poison oak and other toxic plants prevent you from getting in to work. A goat may be staked out on a rope to forage on a specific area, or you can fence in a large bushy area and let the goats clean it out. It's essential to remove the goats just as soon as the area is thinned, because they will start in on the trees before you know it. If you want an area cleaned just once, ask around to borrow one or two goats from a neighbor or farmer.

CHAPTER 8

TWICE THE GARDEN FOR HALF THE PRICE

America is truly a land of plenty, and there is lots of opportunity to garden cheaply or free here. The problem is we've been conditioned to *buy* what we need instead of scrounging around for free stuff. True ingenuity and a bit of hard work yield what there is no money to buy, because necessity is always the mother of invention.

Perhaps the very best source of building materials and decorative pieces for gardens can be found at house-demolition yards. With lumber prices skyrocketing, the value of torn-down homes is growing all the time. Special companies listed under "demolition" or "house demolition" in the Yellow Pages are hired to salvage old buildings. They remove everything usable, from copper plumbing pipe to Victorian gingerbread trim. Windows, doors, cabinets, screens, beams, plumbing fixtures, and hardware, as well as all sorts of wood products, are carefully dismantled and transported to the demolition yard.

There the pieces are sorted so that, for example, all the doors are stored together, usually under a roof so they won't warp. Demolition yards also pick up odd lots of surplus building materials, such as sliding glass doors and large appliances. The rest of the world may call it a junkyard, but to a budget gardener a demolition yard is a treasure trove. Before you go to the yard and get all excited, it's better to know ahead of time what is valuable and what will become more junk waiting to be used in your own backyard.

WOOD

Next time you price landscape timbers or railroad ties, you might be surprised by how expensive they have become. This is in part because of logging regulation, but also because we are in the throes of a gardening boom, and demand is such that suppliers can raise their prices without losing sales. Railroad ties are timbers dipped liberally into creosote and other petroleum-based preservatives. Considerably smaller landscape timbers are treated with chemical preservatives, which smell a lot better but don't hold up nearly as long.

Ties and landscape timbers are used for walls of raised planters, curbs, or step risers where earth contacts wood and rot is likely to occur. Years ago, when it was still available, heart redwood was the preferred outdoor wood type, but it was used for many parts of wood-framed buildings as well. One of the most valuable things you can find at the yard is old redwood beams or thick planks. Go to a lumberyard and ask the salesperson to give you a rundown on redwood, how it feels and looks, so that when you encounter it at the demo yard you know it on sight. Redwood becomes discolored over time, so unless you nick the surface, it may appear identical to pine or other softwoods. Even a beam that is not redwood can be coated with creosote or a similar but less offensive-smelling preservative to extend its life if it's used to retain earth.

Beams and other types of salvage wood are usually bristling with nails the workers don't pull out. Doing it yourself can be quite a job, and if the wood is a plank, removing the nails may split the wood. This is less of a problem with thicker pieces. Bring a hammer or flat-bar nail puller with you, as these residual nails can make it difficult to handle and load the wood.

Demo-yard wood is great for creating a rustic look or building cold frames. Naturally weathered siding turns a new shed into a rustic focal point, or lets it settle into the landscape as though it has been there for decades.

Keep an eye out for special architectural pieces, such as classical columns that once might have supported a front porch. A pair makes a stunning gateway, and with luck you'll come across four of them to create a pergola. Shorter, stout columns make perfect bases for gazing balls, birdbaths, larger bird-houses, and sundials. Finials, those balls or pointed ornaments you see on tops of posts, can dress up unin-teresting fences, gateways, or garden sheds.

Solid-core doors are another won-derful buy, especially if they have unique windows. With a little rein-forcing, some are suitable for outdoor gates, and if you can find some great

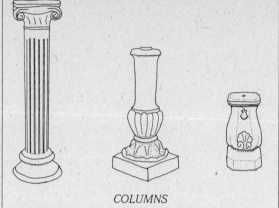

COLUMNS
You may come upon all sorts of columns created from wood, stone, or concrete. The tallest ones are best suited to overhead structures or to use as gar-den ornaments. Shorter, pedestal-shaped pieces are good bases for sundials, birdbaths, or sculpture.

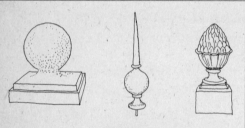

FINIALS
Finials can be made of wood, stone, or con-crete. They top fence posts, balustrades, or newel posts, or simply stand alone to mark edges of terraces and patios. Restored finials can grace the top of a gazebo or garden shed.

old hinges, a normal backyard access be-comes an attractive portal. Solid-core doors also make great potting tables. Some can be cut down into useful planks. Their older round brass knobs are good for crushing herbs in a thick ceramic bowl like a mortar and pestle. If you find the clear or tinted glass knobs, snatch them up. Carefully placed in the garden along with colored electrical glass insulators,

they make beautiful eye catchers when the sun shines through them.

You might also find segments of wood fencing, usually pickets of one sort or another. These need not be used to enclose anything. Those that are highly ornamental make lovely garden backgrounds. For example, if

PICKETS
Fence pickets were created with many different decorative tips, some simple points and others highly ornate. Look for segments of fence or single pickets.

you have a backyard surrounded by a high wood fence, use these picket segments to portion it into smaller spaces where you plant different types of flowers. A quick coat of paint returns the fences to their former glory, but in rustic surroundings even the rust stains from nails add character.

There are often lots of wood shutters at demo yards, too. If you have an unbroken garage wall, create a fake window. Select a nice old window from the yard, repaint it, and nail it sash and all onto the wall. If the wall is light-colored, you may want to paint the inside of the glass black so the garage wall doesn't peek through the window. The select two matching shutters and paint them, too. Nail one up on each side of the window. You might even grow vines on the wall to surround the window. You can create a fake doorway in a similar fashion.

Never be in a hurry when you visit the demo yard, because impulsive purchases often go unused. In your haste you may also pass over that one-in-a-million find that could provide the essential character of your garden. For example, detailing on commercial buildings was once created with ceramic material called architectural terra-cotta. You may find bits and pieces of these works of art that can be built into a masonry wall, added to paving, attached to wood surfaces, or incorporated into a water feature.

METALS

A lot of what you find at the demo yard is made of metal, either decorative or functional. Old buildings were sometimes flashed with copper, or images were worked into bronze friezes. The real value of bronze and copper is that they resist rusting and take on that wonderful green patina that fits so well into gardens.

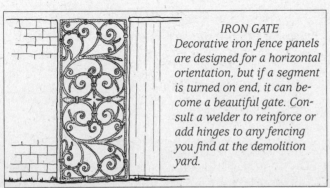

IRON GATE
Decorative iron fence panels are designed for a horizontal orientation, but if a segment is turned on end, it can become a beautiful gate. Consult a welder to reinforce or add hinges to any fencing you find at the demolition yard.

Perhaps the most fun is an old segment of iron fencing. Remember that a fence doesn't always have to enclose something. Highly detailed fencing, such as Victorian cast iron, becomes an artwork in itself as a beautiful background for a fountain, or the suggestion of the edge of a space. Lacy vines such as clematis threading through the patterns add to the beauty. Sections of these fences can even be turned on end: reinforced and hinged, the old iron segment becomes the perfect gate for a 6-foot tall fence or wall.

There are three basic types of old metal fence: wrought-iron, shaped-wire, and cast-iron. Wrought iron is plentiful, holds up well, and can be easily welded. It is simply steel rods worked into permanent patterns. Shaped wire is not so common but was the middle-class standard at the turn of the century. It does not hold up well without reinforcement but is still charming if you can find it. Cast iron is less common and tends to be very heavy. It is notoriously brittle and can rarely be welded because it cracks uncontrollably. Reinforcement must be done by bolting on pieces of steel. Cast-iron pieces are old and frequently rusted through, but salvaging portions for gateways or other creative uses is well worth the effort.

BEER-BUDGET ITEM: If you are building a brick, block, or stone wall, increase the sense of space by making windowlike openings that allow light to penetrate. In Persian gardens, such openings increased air circulation into walled courtyards, and were frequently covered with grillwork of carved wood or metal to ensure security and limit views from the outside. Pieces of old cast-iron fencing or heat registers are perfect for this. Combine grilles with rows of stacked bottles, tiny antique windows, colored-tile fragments, and carved stone so you end up with an artistic statement in addition to a wall. Keep this in mind when you go a-hunting in the demo yard, because these items are often stored as interior items rather than recommended as candidates for garden decoration.

Other things to look for in demo yards include craftsman-style hinges and latches typically used on front doors. These are large and easily bear the weight of wider gates. Handles, drawer pulls, brass thresholds, and containers of beaten copper or

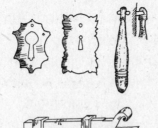

HINGES
Many older doors and gates were built with oversized decorative hinges. They come in all shapes and sizes, with those of the 1920s craftsman period some of the most unusual. Take time to see the beauty beneath a coating of rust, and if you come upon any that are bronze, snatch them up despite the tarnish.

HARDWARE
Keep an eye out for miscellaneous pieces of hardware, which can be made of iron, copper, or bronze. Don't buy a new pull for the gate—find an older, decorative one. Even if you don't have a lock, the metal plates with keyholes can be screwed onto a gate to give the illusion of age. Some demo yards have this sort of hardware all mixed up in bins or barrels. Take time to look at each piece, because underneath the dirt and corrosion you might find some highly ornamental detail.

zinc can all be incorporated into a garden scheme if you are creative. Don't overlook rusted hinges stiff with age. When sanded and oiled, they may surprise you with their beauty.

Many demo yards and local landfills must contend with expired appliances, such as washers and dryers. They usually salvage any recyclable metals, such as copper, but it is the drums that are of most value to gardeners. These sizable, steel-enameled drums make durable containers for raised planters or patio gardens. A washing-machine drum is already perforated with small holes and made of thicker metal than a dryer drum. Paint the outside with mastic or some sort of floor-tile glue—even asphalt emulsion will do—then arrange sticks around the outside and pull them together with baling wire or cable with a turnbuckle, binding them tightly to create a redwood-planter look.

If you're looking for a container for liquid manure, water storage, or simply a sizable planting container, you may find an empty 50-gallon drum at the demo yard. Be sure it does not

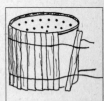

WASHER-DRUM PLANTER
It's not difficult to make a planter out of an old washing-machine drum. First find a drum and remove the agitator if it isn't already gone. Then paint the outside but leave a few of the lowest holes open to ensure drainage. Then finish the outside with sticks, planks, or any other material you have on hand.

contain any toxic residues. To create two trough planters perfect for herbs, have a welder cut the barrel lengthwise into two pieces. These drums also make good trash burners, barbecues, and safe campfire containers.

Old claw-foot bathtubs, some over 6 feet long, are very expensive to renovate if the enamel has been damaged, so they tend to accumulate in demo yards. I recently discovered a gardener who salvaged these tubs and grew an entire vegetable garden in them. Filled with earth they were tall enough to eliminate stooping and were thus ideal for anyone with physical limitations who must garden from a wheelchair or a sitting position.

Heavy cast iron and the protective covering of enamel, however damaged, has an infinite life span even if exposed to water and earth. The slope of the tub guarantees that water accumulates at the end where the drain hole is conveniently located. It's a good idea to line the bottom with pottery shards or large crushed gravel before filling with soil to ensure that there is sufficient drainage overall. For patio gardens, condo living, or even a postage-stamp backyard, claw-foot tubs may be the ultimate gardening solution. The outside can be painted a rich dark green or any decorative color you please. Be aware of the weight, because a tub full of soil, with accumulated water, can be *very* heavy.

METALWORKING SERVICES

For those who have big ideas for metalwork in the garden but aren't prepared to make it a do-it-yourself project, it's wise to hire a professional. The most skilled with all types of metal, from aluminum to cast iron, is the certified welder. Not only are these craftsmen welders, but they can fabricate complex precision parts as well. Certified welders are expensive because of the licensing and training, but you are assured that any job done is first-rate.

To save money on less critical welding projects, take a drive to the country. Anyone who grows up on a working farm today knows how to weld, since so many tasks are mechanized. These barnyard welders work cheaply and do a pretty good job with both oxygen-acetylene and arc for a more than fair price.

The third type of metalworker is a blacksmith; today this skill is performed by horseshoers, technically called farriers. This is the old-time anvil-pounding method

WELDING—THE METAL LOVER'S TOOL

Years ago I took a course in oxygen-acetylene welding and discovered it is a delicate job much like sewing—but a lot hotter! To weld two pieces of metal properly, you must melt both sides equally into a pool of molten metal and move at an even pace while you dip the filler rod. This is not easy, and many inexperienced amateurs tend to melt the filler rod as though it were glue. It may appear correct, but when pressure is applied, the filler is not capable of holding the metals together. If you really want to have fun with outdoor sculpture and creative metalwork, take a course in welding and learn to do it right.

You can also use a torch to cut metal, which requires no special skill. This is more in line with an amateur's ability, but a welding course ensures your own safety and that of bystanders. If you're not careful, you could blind yourself or blow up half the block. A hacksaw is a more laborious but safer way to cut metal. Or consider a Sawsall, which is a big electric power tool that functions like a saber saw. You must put steel blades on it to cut metal, and you can only cut metals of minimal thickness.

of working iron and steel by hand with a forge, and many history buffs are creating period ironwork this way. A horseshoer is mobile and he can come with his forge and tools mounted on a pickup truck. If you want a Western-style motif, a horseshoe gate handle, or something that requires shaping iron, such as distinctive outdoor hinges, consult a shoer or get in touch with your local historical society. You'll find shoers in the Yellow Pages or by contacting the nearest racetrack or riding stable.

AUTO WRECKING YARD FINDS

One common metal salvaged from automobiles and other equipment is the axle. Axles make the very best pry bars for digging rocks and holes, because they are well tempered. You can obtain one cheaply from an auto wrecking yard, then take it to a blacksmith. He will beat one end to a dull point for a nominal fee. These are often thicker, cheaper, and far stronger than pry bars you can buy.

Yet another auto wrecking yard find is hubcaps. They are an unorthodox way to make hanging container gardens. Some styles are deeper than others, so look for the deepest ones you can find. Drill holes around the rims for baling wire to hang them from and pound holes in the middle for drainage. If you don't like the chrome look, paint the outsides black or hunter green. Then plant your garden inside the hubcap.

CONCRETE: THE POOR MAN'S BUILDING BLOCKS

Not long ago I had the pleasure of visiting a friend's home and discovering one of the most innovative ideas for home landscaping I've ever seen. John had come upon the spoils of a warm-pink 1960s patio recently torn out of a nearby yard. He saved the neighbor a trip to the dump and took home the fragments, which averaged about two feet in diameter in irregular shapes. There in his tiny postage-stamp yard John fitted the pieces together on a leveling bed of sand and mortared the joints. When he was through, the warm-pink concrete proved nearly identical to expensive Arizona flagstone, and for little more than the price of mortar and a lot of patience he achieved a stunning result.

This is a perfect example of how versatile concrete can be even after it is torn out. In many places flagstone is simply not available unless shipped in at tremendous cost. But concrete is strong, of even thickness, and widely available. Many older slabs are tinted in various shades, and more than one color can be combined into paving. The fragments do not have to be closely spaced, because they are

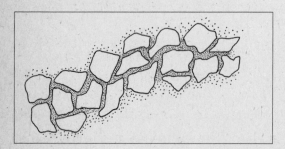 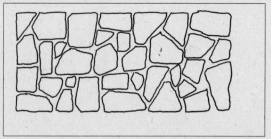

CONCRETE-FRAGMENT PAVING
You can combine fragments of concrete into patios and footpaths. Simply fit the pieces together like a jig-saw puzzle, leaving a small space for mortar or plants. Colored concrete is always more fun to work with than the plain gray material.

 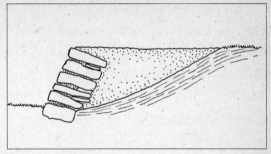

CONCRETE-FRAGMENT CURB WALLS

Because of the consistent thickness of concrete slabs, the fragments can be stacked up into a curb wall. These can be created to hold soil against sloping ground like a miniature retaining wall. The irregular face of the wall will be far more attractive if planted with cascading perennials. The face can also be colored with a concrete stain or a weak paint solution brushed onto the broken edges to better simulate more expensive materials, such as stone.

CONCRETE PLANTER AND STEPPERS

LEFT: *You can build a dry stone wall to create a unique and long-lasting raised planter.* RIGHT: *Irregularly shaped slabs of broken concrete make good lawn stepping-stones. These, too, can be tinted to a more natural tone with concrete stain or paint. Budget gardeners with a little artistic talent can try a faux-marble paint job to mimic more expensive materials. This is a popular treatment these days, and you'll find kits and books on how to paint faux finishes at most craft stores. Simply follow the instructions, but use outdoor paint.*

equally attractive when grass or matlike groundcovers are planted between each piece instead of mortar. They also make good individual stepping-stones.

Concrete pieces can also be used to create curbs and low walls. The even thickness of concrete makes it stack well, leaving only the broken edges on the outside and the finished surface of the top piece visible. Stacking can be used to create a vertical wall up to 2 feet tall, or a step-back wall on a slope. If you build your concrete-piece wall to hold back soil, leave openings between the layers for planting.

An old method of creating a rock garden on a slope is to bury fragments of concrete on end. This creates little benches on a slope for landings, which catch water and funnel it back into the sloping ground. The fragments can be widely spaced or arranged in tight formation, depending on how stable the slope is. For example, sandy soil does not hold together well, so many fragments may be needed to hold it all solidly in place.

You can also use small concrete fragments partially buried on end for edging flowerbeds and lawns. The depth to which you bury the fragment depends on soil conditions, but it must be sufficient to keep the pieces in place even when the earth is wet. Remember that you may be running power equipment around a lawn near this edging, and these pieces must be stable enough to stand up under the wear.

It's not difficult to find broken concrete, but getting it home can be a problem. Concrete is very heavy, and just a few fragments will load down a passenger car. It's better to use a pickup truck or rent a trailer. To find concrete, which is often used as a filler material, contact concrete contractors, general contractors, stonemasons, or landscape contractors. They may be willing to truck the concrete to your house for unloading before they go to the dump, but chances are it will be mixed in with dirt, steel, and other rubbish from the job site. It's better to show up at the site and be ready to collect the best pieces yourself, particularly if you are looking for tinted slabs.

Concrete isn't the only waste material that can be used in gardens. Broken bricks, pavers, and concrete blocks are also versatile, and combined with concrete flagstones, they create a far more interesting effect. Inquire at masonry supply yards for these items. Sometimes you can buy odd lots for next to nothing. One of my clients ordered a shipment of Mexican glazed tile, and the entire load was so poorly fired that the glaze chipped right off. That tile supplier had to take it back and was eager to sell it at bargain-basement prices to make room in his warehouse. You may also find plenty of broken masonry units left over from jobs in smaller quantities. These can be had cheap or free if you request them from the warehouse and pick them up yourself.

Whenever there is a tiler or a stonemason on a construction site, there are bound to be waste materials lying around that are great for crazy-quilt paving. Yet another source is swimming-pool contractors, who carry a variety of water-line tiles and coping units. Most of this type of tile is frostproof, an important feature for some outdoor projects. Products are continually being phased out as new ones are introduced, which causes tons of samples to be discarded. The large tiles make excellent trivets, and the midsize ones are perfect coasters after you glue a layer of matching felt to the bottom for cushioning. Anyone who doubts how valuable these freebies can be should take a look at the Watts Towers, a Los Angeles landmark created entirely of mortar and waste tile.

Stepping-stones are always useful in the garden, particularly near hose bibs, where we risk crushing plants as we step into a planter to turn on the water. They are great in lawns, too, along frequently traveled routes where the battered turf never seems to grow in properly. For a unique and inexpensive solution, consider paver tiles that average about a foot square. Odd lots, samples, or low-quality tiles can be had for pennies if not for free, but some will need a support to keep them from breaking under your body weight.

Terra-cotta tiles called Saltillo pavers are made in Mexico; priced dirt-cheap, they have a natural coloring that fits nicely into garden settings. Since they are not particularly durable and will break under the slightest weight, support these and other tiles with a stronger base material such as concrete.

If the tile or pavers are flat enough, you can simply glue them to an old stepping-stone or a square piece of wood for support. But for warped or uneven pieces, simply press each one into a base of wet concrete, which will mold to the irregular shape. Once the concrete dries, the tile will probably pop off, but the impression will remain. Apply mastic to the impression and replace the tile, pressing it down firmly. Once the mastic is completely dried, you have a unique and inexpensive custom stepping-stone.

A cheap and easy way to create a form for your wet concrete base is to use a shallow cardboard box from a case of beer. If you are working with smaller tiles, you'll be able to fit quite a few into a single box-sized base. For larger single tiles, cut the box down to slightly larger than the tile with scissors or a knife and reinforce the new edges with duct tape. These forms hold up only for a single pour, so have a separate box for each stepping-stone you plan to make.

To begin, simply mix up your concrete in a wheelbarrow and pour it carefully into the first box. Use the flat edge of a board to screed off the excess and flatten the surface so it is as level as possible. Then press down the paver or tile while the concrete is fresh before you go on to the second box, and so on. Allow the concrete to set for a day or two, then tear away the cardboard. Although these forms are not the most precise way to accomplish the job, they never seem to look out of place once in the garden.

OTHER STUFF THAT'S CHEAP OR FREE

No one wants to see the garden hose unless it is being used. You can buy a ceramic terra-cotta hose pot, but at $50 to $100, this is certainly not a beer-budget item. Sometimes home-improvement stores will have great sales on half-oak barrels, which for less money are perfect for holding the hose, and their natural wood coloring blends into the landscape.

VENETIAN BLINDS

You may know these as mini-blinds, made of either plastic or painted metal. The older models with wider slats were common in schools and office buildings and are quite well made. There are lots of uses for the slats in the garden, and if the strings on your blinds at home break and it's not worth repairing them, you have a great garden resource. The slats from less-expensive plastic mini-blinds, which are only about an inch wide, make ideal plant labels, such as those nurseries stick into a pack of annual seedlings to identify what variety they are. These plastic slats can be easily cut with scissors so that one end is pointed and slides into your seed trays. Use a permanent marker or a grease pencil to write on the labels. They are also perfect for marking the varieties of shrubs, perennials, and roses in the landscape, since they do not decompose. And since they are made from waste products, you can throw the old ones away.

Longer segments of the old-style 2.5-inch-wide metal blinds stand up more stiffly than the plastic and can be used in flats or other containers as dividers. Simply cut them with tin snips to the desired length and push the edge about an inch into the soil. In the garden they can enclose the edges of creeping plants to keep them within a confined area.

GLASS OR CERAMIC INSULATORS

Don't you hate it when the garden hose smashes plants when you pull on it? You can buy "hose guides," but there's another cheap or free alternative. Glass insulators, which once sat on power poles all across America, are out of use today, but they show up at garage sales and junk stores. With their blue and green coloring, so iridescent in the sunlight, they make beautiful and unusual hose guides. Each insulator was once screwed onto a threaded wooden spindle on the power pole, which is why the inside of each one was cast with threads. This empty core allows an insulator to be securely set upon a wood anchor stake pounded into the earth. A broom handle is perfectly sized, and the insulator can be glued snugly in place with silicone or hot glue. Simply push these staked insulators into the soil at key points for the garden hose, then enjoy their beautiful color.

Modern insulators are more often made of ceramic material with a brown shiny glaze. These have shapes that function even better as hose guides and can be very large. Attach an anchor stake to these and place them at strategic points in your garden.

BURLAP BAGS

If you have access to burlap bags, by all means gather them up. They provide a perfect way to grow potatoes, because unlike plastic bags they allow plenty of air exchange and ideal drainage. This is a good method when you don't have enough room to devote to potatoes in the garden. Simply fill a bag up with good soil and plant your seed pieces in the top. An alternative method is to fill the bag with soil and tie the end closed tightly with baling wire or rope. Lay the bag down on its side and cut small holes in the middle to plant the potatoes. Place your burlap potato bags in a sunny

BURLAP-BAG POTATO PLANTERS
Never throw away a burlap bag. Instead, use it as a potato planter that is guaranteed to grow great spuds. Other root crops also like this method, because of the soft texture of potting soil with no dense clay layers or rocks.

place and keep them moist. By the time they are ready for harvest, the burlap will be decomposing and you need only cut it open and gather the spuds. This method may also work for other root or leaf crops, such as carrots or beets.

CABLE SPOOLS

Wood cable spools make ideal garden tables that will stand up to severe weather. It's not hard to find the large, wood cable spools used by utility companies or the contractors that do work for them. Call around to power companies, telephone companies, and cable television companies, as well as mechanical contractors and cable-supply wholesalers, and chances are you'll find one. The hard part is getting a good-sized spool home, because they are heavy and a pickup truck is needed to move one. But there are smaller versions, which are easier to transport and make convenient outdoor end tables.

BUCKETS

Few items are more useful to gardeners than a good stout bucket with a tight-fitting lid. The best ones are those used by bakeries to hold pie fillings and the like. My local supermarket bakery sells used buckets for just a dollar apiece. Not only are they ideal for storage, but they are good containers to carry small tools and supplies as you go about your gardening tasks.

SEWING MACHINES

If you find a rusty treadle sewing machine base at the junkyard, don't pass it up. These cast iron bases make beautiful outdoor tables once cleaned up and painted. A simple wood top—either left natural and sealed, or painted with weather-resistant paint—is perfect beside a bentwood chair or chaise longue.

SUNFLOWERS

Big sunflowers are popular motifs these days, and you find them on everything from dishes to dresses. Sunflowers are one of the easiest crops to

SUNFLOWER BIRD FEEDER Never go out and buy a bird feeder—grow one for pennies. Be sure to buy seed for "mammoth" sunflowers, as there are some newer hybrids that are much smaller.

grow where there is plenty of sunshine. Mature flowers make beautiful bird feeders: simply tie twine to the flowers, and hang them from tree branches all around your garden. Add some wild bird food to this flat, dishlike surface and the birds will hang around.

MILITARY SURPLUS—A VIRTUAL GOLD MINE

Perhaps the greatest untapped supply of great gardening stuff is the U.S. Military, and you can find most of the following items in army-surplus stores. Individuals who buy and sell surplus military stuff often set up booths at "gun shows," held from time to time in some communities, and they have some of the best prices in town.

If there isn't a military-surplus store near you, write or call for the free U.S. Cavalry catalog, which carries a full line of military clothing and equipment. (U.S. Cavalry, 2855 Centennial Ave, Radcliff, KY 40160-9000; phone (800) 333-5102). You'll also find similar clothing sold in the Gander Mountain catalog, which is used by hunters. Gander Mountain, Box 248, Hwy. W, Wilmont, WI 53192; phone (800) 558-9410.

FATIGUE PANTS

Army fatigues make ideal gardening pants, comparable to or perhaps better than their commercial counterparts, which can be quite pricey. In fact, fatigues must be sold as "used" when they've been worn just a few times, and many supply outlets sell used clothing ranging in quality from just this side of tattered to nearly new. Take your time, and chances are you'll come across some pretty good deals.

The great big pockets on the outside of each leg are ideal for carrying clippers and other bulky items such as seed packets or bulbs. The pockets can be securely buttoned closed, and you can fit a surprising amount in them because of the outside pleat. Because fatigues are designed to be worn with taller boots, pant legs run on the short side, which keeps the bottoms out of the mud, and many styles have a drawstring around the cuff, which, if pulled tight, prevents bugs from crawling up your legs. The seat and knees are reinforced with a double layer of fabric. The loose fit allows a maximum range of movement. You can turn fatigues into roomy summer gardening shorts and still retain many of the neat features. Simply cut them off just below the reinforced seam at the bottom of the pockets and they'll hold up indefinitely.

FIELD JACKETS

Field jackets are loose-fitting jackets that are fairly long, reaching well below the waist. This makes them comfortably roomy even with a sweater on underneath, and when you bend over, the jacket doesn't ride up and expose your lower back. Field jackets also feature large pleated pockets to carry your gardening gloves, plant-tie tape, bulbs, and clippers.

BOOTS

The part-canvas jungle boots used in Vietnam are designed to allow air exchange in moist conditions, perfect for the warmer months. All sorts of insulated boots are excellent for winter tasks, when knee-high rubber boots just aren't warm enough or cause your socks to slide down into a big knot. You'll also find quality leather boots that are resistant to snakebite, good for rural gardeners working in the brush.

GLOVES

If you're like most gardeners, you spend a lot of time trying to find gloves you took off and left somewhere outdoors. Many of the knit military gloves sell for just a dollar or two per pair and are reinforced with leather or plastic. At this low price you can afford to keep a few pairs on hand so you don't spend so much time hunting down the lost ones. The military also makes neoprene gloves similar to wetsuit gloves used by divers. Although they aren't cheap, these are wonderful for winter cold or wet weather, because they insulate your hands and keep them dry and their sticky touch ensures a secure grip.

Tank camouflage and parachutes

To shade a hot patio, most people either wait for a tree to grow or build an expensive shade arbor. But a permanent shade structure can block sunlight and make interior rooms dark in winter, when sun is most appreciated. As we saw in Chapter 6, this does not promote energy conservation. A cheap military alternative is a tank cover, basically a large sheet of earth-tone jute netting with strips of camouflage fabric woven in and out of the holes. Because a tank is so large, it takes a huge piece of this stuff to conceal it. You can use a tank cover to create a summertime awning for patios by attaching two corners to the building and the other two corners to temporary support poles. You can also increase the shading potential of arbors or trellis structures out in the landscape in this way without adding much weight. Tank covers go up in the spring and come down for the winter.

A parachute can be used the same way, and newer models are rectangular, a shape that lends itself to this use better than the older, round ones. The advantage to parachutes is that they are lighter in weight than tank-camo netting, so the support posts or eye bolts need not be as sturdy. Because of their filmy nature, parachutes don't offer dense shade, but they do provide a graceful, almost luxurious effect.

Ammo boxes

Military ammunition boxes are made of strong steel, open from the top, and can be closed securely and locked. Very large types hold shells for tanks, tiny ones for handguns. All can be bought for $3 to $10 apiece, depending on the size. They are ideal for holding toxic garden chemicals that should be locked away from children. Some are fairly airtight and can be used to store seed and other sensitive materials that must stay as dry as possible.

CREATIVE GARDENING IDEAS FOR ALL SORTS OF STUFF

Over the years gardeners have come up with many ingenious ideas for using common items. Here are some that we have not covered in the previous chapters.

1. Never spend money on tree sealer if you have interior latex paint left over. This is a popular way to seal large cuts on trees, shrubs, and roses to reduce moisture loss and discourage entry of pests. If the color is white, paint the tender trunks of small trees, which are vulnerable to sunscald.

2. Inner tubes, particularly those from ten-speed bicycles, make excellent ties to secure trees to a support stake. You can slice automobile inner tubes into giant rubber bands, which have dozens of uses.

3. An old baby buggy or a red wagon can function as a garden cart.

4. Plastic picnic knives, with the names of plants written in black waterproof marker, are excellent row or seedling labels.

5. Use cloth nail aprons to carry all your small tools or seed packets during planting time. Many hardware stores give these out free of charge as a promotional item or sell them for a dollar or so. Compare this with the cost of similar "official" gardening tool belts and you'll be surprised at the difference.

6. Don't throw away wire coat hangers because they make a fine structure for topiary forms. Simply bend one or more coat hangers into the desired shape, straighten the hook, and push it into garden soil. Plant dwarf ivy and train it to the skeleton shape and soon it will completely cover the wire. Coat hangers also make good stakes, pins, and other hold-fasts around the garden.

CHAPTER 9

THE MIRACLES OF MAIL ORDER

What publication has the vivid color of *Architectural Digest*, the information content of *National Geographic*, the wide selection of the *Sears Wish Book*, and the how-to guidance of *Popular Mechanics*, all for the price of the Sunday *New York Times*? It's any one of today's first-class gardening catalogs. Busy lifestyles limit how much time we have to drive to the mall, find a parking space, and fight the crowds. The preference for the selection, prices, and convenience of armchair shopping is spilling over into the gardening market in a very big way.

There are still more advantages to shopping for plants by mail. When you visit the garden center, you'll be drawn to plants that are blooming and labeled with only the genus, species, or common name. Rarely do the displays provide any growing information or detail special needs a plant might have. As a result you risk choosing a plant not suited to your garden, and when it dies you lose money.

In contrast, a good color catalog shows you plants in bloom for every season at once, and each variety is usually described in detail. There may be tips and instructions throughout the catalog, which help you to become a better gardener and save you the cost of how-to gardening books. In catalogs such as the *Tomato Growers Supply*, you'll find even more in-depth information on growing this favorite food crop than you would in a more general catalog. Best of all, you can catalog-shop all year round, when it snows, on rainy days, and even when the ground is frozen. Interest in plant catalogs is always greater during the winter months, when gardens are dormant.

But there are disadvantages to catalog shopping as well, and being aware of the limitations allows you to make smarter choices. Inspired by all the lavish color and huge selection, many people tend to overbuy, which sometimes results in wasted dollars and dead or neglected plants. Also keep in mind that some plants are better suited for transit than others. For example, shipping a bare-root fruit tree is a bit more difficult than shipping a neat little box of tulip bulbs. This is not to say the tree isn't a good choice, but the cost of shipping and any damage that occurs in transit are likely to raise the price of this plant and reduce its vigor compared with those of a bare root sold locally.

THE PROS AND CONS OF MAIL-ORDER PLANTS

Pros	Cons
Better selection	Popular varieties may sell out early
Convenient shopping	No way to handpick your plant from those available
Informative catalogs	May exaggerate size and vigor of plants listed
Color photos	Don't always represent true nature of the plant under normal garden conditions
Lower prices	Addition of shipping costs to price
Home delivery	Trauma during shipping—heat, cold, breakage, dehydration
	Size of plants limited to constraints of shipping
	Cost of printing lavish catalog may be passed on to customer

MAIL-ORDER CAVEATS

Not all mail-order nurseries are the same. In fact, there are a good number of them that deceive customers with their advertisements. For example, a special offer advertising a "mole and gopher repelling plant" for only $5 gave no reference at all to the genus and species of this plant, but one glance at the color photo proved it was a common oleander. Certainly it is poison to burrowing rodents, but it's also highly toxic to people and pets, yet this threat was not mentioned at all in the ad. Moreover, oleanders are so common they sell for pennies at local nurseries, where you get a wide choice of flower colors. Since entire catalogs can be written with just this sort of misleading information, it is essential to do business only with reputable companies. Otherwise, you may be duped into buying something by mail for a higher price than you would pay locally.

TWO EXAMPLES OF MISLEADING MAIL-ORDER "SPECIALS"

GIANT WHITE SKYSCRAPER SWEET CORN

One package of *ten* seeds costs a whopping $3.95. All varieties of sweet corn in the *Burpee Catalog*, a reputable supplier, are priced at only $1.35 for *200* seeds. Also, there is a reason why mainstream suppliers don't carry some varieties: It never really reaches this size, the corn kernels are tough and fibrous, it isn't that sweet, or the variety is susceptible to diseases, such as smut.

CLIMBING SPAGHETTI SQUASH

Here is a common variety of winter squash advertised as a climbing plant, but any experienced gardener knows that this squash is too heavy to be trained vertically as a vine. The ad offers us one set of six plants for $5.95, probably newly germinated seedlings, although the age is not specified. Burpee's spaghetti squash seed sells at $1.15 for *25* seeds. Besides, of all veggie garden plants, squash are some of the quickest and easiest to germinate.

IMPORTANT BUYING TIPS AND RESOURCES

It's always a good idea to shop prices of mail-order plants or equipment just as you would any other retail source, but it's hard to comparison-shop without several similar catalogs on hand. Acclaimed as the best source book on the subject, *Gardening by Mail*, by Barbara Barton, in its 4th updated edition, is a virtual bible on the subject and contains more than 2,500 listings. The money you invest in buying the book will be offset many times over by the numerous cheap or free catalogs you can order. And if you don't end up buying anything from the catalogs, refer to the end of this chapter for ideas on recycling and making crafts from dated issues.

Just as other industries have associations that establish standards, the Mailorder Association of Nurseries is a group of the nation's most well known catalog plant sellers. Members can be relied upon for their truth in advertising, customer service, and quality products, though not all quality nurseries are members, so don't dismiss one just because it isn't found on this roster. A detailed listing of members is found in the association's booklet entitled *The Complete Guide to Gardening and Landscaping by Mail*. You may obtain one by sending $2 to the Mailorder Association of Nurseries, PO Box 2129, Dept MEG, Columbia, MD 21045. The booklet also contains helpful hints on buying plants through the mail. If you make a mistake or omit important information, you may end up paying extra or receive a replacement plant not suited to your garden. Here are ten of the most important tips for smart mail-order shopping:

1. Read the catalog descriptions carefully before buying to be sure you are ordering exactly what you want and that the plants are suited to your climate.
2. Fill out the order blank clearly and completely. Don't forget a street address for UPS deliveries, zip code, tax, and shipping charges if requested.
3. When placing an order by phone, keep a record of your order number and the name of the company representative that took your order.
4. If the item you have ordered is sold out, state clearly whether or not you will accept a substitution.
5. Order early in the season to avoid the disappointment of sold-out items.
6. If you require a specific delivery date, state so clearly.
7. Keep a record or a copy of your order and never send cash through the mail.
8. Check for and understand the company's guarantee policy.
9. When the order is delivered, check to make sure it's complete.
10. Plant your new purchases as soon as possible. If something fails to grow, notify the nursery company immediately.

BEER-BUDGET BUYS BY MAIL

Although you can purchase virtually any type of plant by mail, some ship better than others. Sometimes you get a much bigger plant for far less money at a local

SOME QUALITY GENERAL-PURPOSE
SEED COMPANIES

Burgess Seed & Plant Co., Burpee, Clyde Robin Seed Co., DeGiorgi Seed Co., Farmer Seed & Nursery Co., Henry Field's, Gardener's Choice, Gurney's, Harris Seeds, Ed Hume Seeds Inc., Johnny's Selected Seeds, Jung Seed Co., McFayden Seeds, Moon Mountain, Park Seed, W. H. Perron, Stokes Seeds, Territorial Seed Co., Thompson & Morgan.

garden center than by mail, depending, of course, on your location. And if your time is valuable, the special care needed to nurse a traumatized mail-order perennial through transplant shock may prove more expensive than paying an extra dollar or two to buy a big, thriving plant locally.

SEEDS

Seeds will always be the best budget buy, because the flat packages ship easily without risk or bulky packaging. Growing annuals and some perennials from seed costs you just pennies per plant, while that same variety may cost you up to $5 in a gallon-sized container. There is always interest in new varieties that are more disease- and pest-resistant, and these take a while to catch on with commercial growers. With mail order you get a crack at them right from the start, and some seed companies will send free test seeds with your order.

America's eating habits are turning to healthful foods, and many of them can be cultivated in the home vegetable plot. When the economic pinch is being felt at the grocery store, growing a modern-day victory garden makes a lot of sense. For pennies, food plants supply us with completely organic produce in a wide choice of cultivars not carried in stores. The heritage variety trend is strong in edible plants too, and many catalogs offer generous descriptions of each variety. Some, such as Native Seed/SEARCH, concentrate on varieties of food plants cultivated for centuries by the Navajo, Hopi, and many other tribes of the desert Southwest and northern Mexico. Blue corn, black peppers, and desert melons are just a few that

---

SOME UNUSUAL GOURMET SEED AND FOOD-CROP CATALOGS

DeGiorgi Seeds, Native Seed/SEARCH, Pinetree Garden Seeds, Ronniger's Seed Potatoes, Seeds Savers Exchange, Shepherd's Garden Seeds, The Cook's Garden, Tomato Growers Supply Co.

---

allow you to taste history and take advantage of these drought- and disease-resistant plants for no more than the minimal price of a seed packet.

SOME ADVANTAGES TO GROWING FROM SEED:

1. You get to choose *exactly* the flower color you want. Among the many petunias, for example, are single, double, and ruffled fancy flower shapes. Colors range from deep purple to every shade of pink to pure white. There are even striped petal strains. At the garden center you might find just one or two colors or a mixture, whereas the Thompson & Morgan catalog lists more than 25 different varieties.

2. You can buy *lots* of plants for just a couple of dollars. Nursery-grown seedlings start at 25 to 50 cents each. For the price of one or two seedlings, you can buy an entire package of seed. Park Seed, a well-respected national seed-catalog company, offers lettuce seed for about $1.25 per packet, with each packet containing up to *700* seeds. At this price, assuming all the seeds are planted and germinate, you pay .17 cent per head of mature lettuce!

3. You don't have to plant the seed right away, and some types store indefinitely if kept in a dark, dry place. Just ask any Egyptologist about the viability of seed found in pharaohs' tombs after thousands of years. The key in both instances is storing the seed at cool temperatures in a dry, sealed container.

FLOWER BULBS

Flower bulbs are naturally packaged into neat little units that ship easily at any time of year. In most cases it takes a lot of bulbs to create a dramatic planting, so

SOME QUALITY BULB COMPANIES

Breck's, Cooley's Gardens, Dixondale Farms, Dutch Gardens, McClure & Zimmerman, Michigan Bulb Co., Roris Gardens, Shreiner's Iris Gardens, Van Bourgondien Bros., Van Dyck's Flower Farms, Inc., Veldheer Tulip Gardens, Inc.

quantity is critical. Buying a lot of bulbs in the little net bags from the garden center can cost quite a sum, but the Van Bourgondien catalog offers quantities of 50 or 100 for a considerable volume discount.

When you buy bulbs from a quality catalog supplier, not only do you get an incredible choice, but you can also be sure they will be shipped directly to you as quickly as possible. Bearded iris and onions are also sold as bare rootlike bulbs and make excellent mail-order bargains. Bulb companies are eager to satisfy you and make an extra effort to send you fresh bulbs.

ROSES

Roses, like seeds and bulbs, are a massive group of plants with hundreds of varieties ranging from the ancient species to today's most flamboyant hybrid tea roses. The best way to buy a rose is bare root while the plant is leafless and dormant. This makes roses, as well as other bare-root plants, very easy to ship, but only at certain times of year. Retail garden centers usually stock quite a few bare-root rose varieties. The problem for most people is that in this leafless state every one appears virtually identical; a catalog can help you see exactly what you'll be getting.

SOME QUALITY ROSE COMPANIES

Antique Rose Emporium, Heirloom Old Garden Roses, Jackson & Perkins, Roses of Yesterday and Today, The Roseraie at Bayfields.

> **BEER-BUDGET ITEMS:** Virtually any shrub, tree, or vine that is deciduous can be sold bare-root and in that state will ship easily. Bare-root season is during winter or early spring, depending on the region. You will always get a better deal on a plant bare-root because you don't have to pay for the pot and soil.

GARDEN SUPPLIES AND RELATED STUFF

There are a number of very beautiful catalogs that offer all sorts of garden-related items, from tools to clothing. If you can't find similar equipment for sale locally, then the catalogs are a good bet. But if you compare prices between local alternatives and some of the juicy gifts, books, and sundries that fill the catalogs, you'll be surprised at the differences. And don't forget shipping costs! Sending a heavy concrete fountain or brass sundial UPS can add up to quite a bill, and if there is a sales tax in your state the final tally may be heart-stopping. The same applies to large tools such as shovels and pole pruners, which may not be unusually heavy but are difficult to ship because of their unwieldy size. Perhaps it is best to peruse these catalogs for ideas rather than with the intent to buy. You'll find some beer-budget alternatives to many of these products throughout this book.

But there are some other good reasons for ordering and enjoying these catalogs, even though they may be too pricey for budget gardeners. Artists spend a tremendous amount of time and effort designing these catalogs, and you, the consumer, may benefit from their skills.

Here are a few inspirational thoughts on great ideas that can be found on the pages of these catalogs:

1. Attractive combinations of decorative containers and bulbs to force indoors.
2. Gardner's aprons you can design and sew at home to keep handy your gloves, pruning shears, seed packages, and tools.
3. Ugly or forgotten baskets resurrected as gift containers with attractive decorative paint jobs.

4. Designs for simple rustic wall trellises to make with next year's winter prunings.

5. Simple shapes you can weave out of stiff wire for armature topiary forms to support a covering of "Needlepoint" dwarf ivy.

6. Bundles of dried flowers, grasses, and foliage plants decorated with attractive ribbon, twine, or rope.

7. Dried aromatic herbs and foliage to fashion into cook's wreaths or swags.

8. Ways to use berries, bark, and other garden by-products for decorative interior accents.

9. Vine runners for rustic core material in garlands.

10. Dozens of suggestions for garden crops that make great wreaths.

11. Botanical pomander balls that go beyond the traditional clove-and-orange by using moss, lichens, and other common materials.

12. Winter crafts to make with the leftover straw not used in the summer garden.

13. Outdoor birdseed ornaments to attract wildlife.

14. Luminarias that not only glow but can also be cut in attractive patterns.

15. Old galvanized buckets painted a glossy hunter green for French florist's pots.

Before you discard an outdated catalog, particularly one of those that deal in specific types of plants, cut out all the blocks of how-to-grow information. Paste these onto paper and create a gardening file or binder that you can refer to time and again. The same applies to recipes in kitchen garden catalogs, particularly those that describe how to create low-fat vegetable and salad dishes, or even how to cook edible flowers. Add to these information files clips from home-improvement or gardening magazines before you throw them out as well.

SOME QUALITY GARDEN-SUPPLY COMPANIES

Gardener's Eden, Gardener's Supply Company, Kinsman Company, A.M. Leonard, Inc., MacKenzie Nursery Supply, Inc., Smith & Hawken.

CHAPTER 10

WHERE TO GET FREE OR
LOW-COST SERVICES

Private detectives and journalists are trained to find out information about people. They know where records are kept and how routine activities such as paying a telephone bill can produce a wealth of information. Government offices and archives, the public library, corporate records, and computer files all store vital information on virtually every aspect of our daily lives. There is a considerable amount of information out there, but you have to know where to find it. You may be pleasantly surprised at just how much booty you can obtain over the phone or through the mail from both public and private sources.

GOVERNMENT RESOURCES

Government, from the federal level down to your city offices, is a massive resource, which your taxes have supported over the years. Some government agencies produce a tremendous amount of literature that is available free or for a nominal fee. A sizable portion of this is related to agriculture, forestry, wildlife, and other aspects of land management. Each agency—be it federal, state, county, city, or community—produces its own publications.

UNITED STATES DEPARTMENT OF AGRICULTURE

Today there are dozens of agencies that are part of the USDA, including the U.S. Forest Service and the Soil Conservation Service. The USDA has always published informative literature to educate farmers about new agricultural trends, plant diseases, improved cultivars, and livestock care. The publications may be a single sheet, a pamphlet, or a sizable book.

All USDA publications fall into one of the following groups. Some of these are also distributed or sold by state agencies, so you may find some duplication of titles. Most of the USDA Soil Conservation Service publications are classified by category abbreviations:

* *Farmer's Bulletins (FB)* Current how-to information for farmers and ranchers
* *Home and Garden Bulletins (HG)* Subjects for the general public on gardening, agriculture, food, nutrition, and suburban living
* *Leaflets (L)* Brief versions of farmer's bulletins
* *Program Aids (PA)* Updates on government-agency activities to keep the public informed of changes
* *Agriculture Information Bulletins (AIB)* Agriculture information for rural and urban residents, but no how-to information
* *Agriculture Handbooks (AH)* Professional and technical information for those experienced in farming, ranching, or other aspects of agriculture
* *Miscellaneous Publications (MP)* Material not easily classified, at various prices

It is difficult to obtain a catalog of USDA publications, and not everything available is listed there. The most reliable source for consumers is found in the state offices of these federal agencies. There you'll find information specific to your state, region, and immediate locale.

Another approach is to order the *Subject Bibliography Index: A Guide to U.S. Government Publications*. For a free copy, write to Superintendent of Documents, U.S. Government Printing Office, Washington, DC 20402. This reference booklet lists the *subjects* and corresponding code numbers to help you find specific books or brochures. For example, to find U.S. government publications about agriculture, the subject code indicated in the *Subject Bibliography Index* is 162. You then order 162, which is a separate booklet that contains all you need to know about publications in that category. Among the subjects included that could relate to gardening are Agriculture/162, Aquatic Life/209, Birds/177, Environmental Protection/88, The Home/41, Insects/34, Pest and Weed Control/227, Trees, Forest Management and Products/86, Wildlife Management/116.

Obtaining publications from the U.S. Government Printing Office in Washington can be a long, frustrating task. The list is frequently updated, with new titles and price changes. It's much easier to hike down to the public library where they keep a current copy of the publications catalog on file in the reference section. From there you can make choices and easily send for the most up-to-date information.

USDA SOIL CONSERVATION SERVICE (SCS)

One of the least-known yet most important agencies is the USDA Soil Conservation Service, which has at least one office in almost every state. Local offices are listed in the federal government section of the telephone book under U.S. Government, Department of Agriculture. This agency was originally developed to assist farmers in reducing soil erosion. Poor farming practices in the nineteenth and early twentieth centuries contributed to tremendous topsoil losses, which concerned the government enough for it to create an agency to help reduce the problem. Today the SCS is still concerned with soil loss, but it takes an active role in various aspects of environmental protection and emergency assistance after wildfire, dust storms, floods, and earthquakes.

Although part of a federal agency, each office of the SCS is familiar with *local* conditions. The staff is trained to assist private landowners with plant- and soil-related issues such as erosion-control planting and selection of woodlot trees. They are highly skilled in pond design, overseeing construction and maintenance to make sure farmers and rural homeowners create water bodies that are safe and successful over the long term. They will also evaluate a piece of property to determine what kind of wildlife it supports and make suggestions for suitable cover and food plants.

Unfortunately, the duties of this agency are increasing while their funding declines, limiting the number of field agents on staff. To request assistance, give the nearest office a call and explain your situation. If they feel it is warranted, the agent will make an appointment to visit your site or homesite. You may also visit the office, where hundreds of fact sheets are kept on file. These are free for the asking, and since they are specific to your immediate area or region, they are far more valuable than general agricultural publications.

The SCS publishes a series of plant sheets that covers the management and uses of many species of garden plants, from grasses to trees. They also offer job sheets, which discuss projects such as erosion-control planting or the creation of windbreaks. Still other publications include agricultural information bulletins, home and garden bulletins, and education-oriented program aids, which are terrific resources. There are also sheets on how to install or maintain irrigation systems of all types. The SCS files include detailed reference information that has been gathered over many years. The staff will help you find what you need and copy anything that covers your particular subject matter.

EXAMPLES OF DIFFERENT TITLES THAT FALL UNDER THE LOOSE HEADINGS OF SCS PLANT AND JOB SHEETS

Plant sheets:
Management and Uses of Western Red Cedar
Management and Uses of Desert Willow
Management and Uses of English Ivy
Management and Uses of Chokecherry

Job sheets:
Cover and Green-Manure Crops
How to Use Multiflora Rose
How to Plant a Tree
Preserving Natural Vegetation
Temporary Erosion Control on Newly Reshaped Slopes

Following are general USDA titles that may be of interest to gardeners, accompanied by the *current* document numbers. They are organized according to the nine headings described above. All are free except those indicated by a price.

Agriculture Information Bulletins

AIB 223   Grass Makes Its Own Food
AIB 513   Soil Erosion by Water
AIB 555   Soil Erosion by Wind

Agriculture Handbooks

AH 170   Grass Varieties in the United States

Home and Garden Bulletins

HG 179   Gardening on the Contour
HG 185   Mulches for Your Garden

Leaflets

L 557   Maintaining Subsurface Drains
L 570   Farming and Maintaining Terraces

Program Aids

PA 1093   Invite Birds to Your Home: Conservation Plantings for the Southeast
PA 1094   Invite Birds to Your Home: Conservation Plantings for the Northwest
PA 1352   Assistance Available from the Soil Conservation Service
PA 1408   "Rodan" Western Wheatgrass
PA 1411   "Cimarron" Little Bluestem

STATE GOVERNMENT

In 1914 Congress passed legislation to create the nationwide Cooperative Extension program as part of the land-grant university in every state. It involves three levels of government that share funding for this service, a support system for agriculture, natural resources development, and consumer science. At the federal level, USDA provides some support, at the statewide level the university system contributes, and individual counties organize educational programs and literature specific to local needs. Also involved are the Farm, Home and Youth Advisors, which organizes activities connected with 4-H clubs and county fairs. The Cooperative Extension is really a clearinghouse for accurate information and is the central office for field agents who specialize in livestock and crop farming.

These agents are part of the university system and are well trained in their fields. Unfortunately, they are too few to serve the general public, so they primarily deal with farmers, although the livestock experts will advise you by phone. To lighten the workload of agents, the Master Gardener program was developed to connect experienced gardeners with those who are seeking answers to questions about home landscapes. The Master Gardener is put through a technical training program free of charge and in return is required to donate a specific number of hours to helping the public. The MGs are in the office at certain times to answer questions by phone, and some may even be willing to visit your home. For example, if you wish to plant a home orchard, or maybe just a few fruit trees, it's important to know what varieties grow best in your area, and whether or not a second pollinating tree is needed. A call to the Master Gardener is all it takes to obtain this information free of charge—and best of all, you can be sure it is accurate and up to date.

Your Cooperative Extension office is the best and most accessible place to find inexpensive government publications on home, garden, and farming. You'll find the extension office listed in the phone book under County Department of Agriculture and/or Farm Advisor.

Some states sell Cooperative Extension publications, which are great low-priced and sometimes free resources. You can obtain a catalog listing publications and their prices by calling the extension office and requesting one. The catalog contains a list of publications available for your state, including descriptions and prices. Most are $1 to $3, although there are some more expensive books that cover specific subjects in greater depth. Some are federal publications, some are written on a state level, and still more are specific to your immediate area. The following are examples of booklets on gardening subjects you may find in such a catalog:

- *Irises for the Home Gardener*, 40 pp., $1.50
- *Aphids in the Home Garden and Landscape*, 8 pp., $1.50
- *Gypsum and Other Chemical Amendments for Soil Improvement*, 8 pp., $1.50
- *The Rapid Composting Method*, 4 pp., $1.50
- *Lawn Aeration and Thatch Control*, 4 pp., $1.50

You'll find many more titles that indirectly relate to gardening and cover subjects you won't find anywhere else, such as protection of trees on construction sites, canning and preserving, wildlife and plant field guides, fruit and vegetable production, raising livestock and poultry, water quality, and even guidelines for managing your own woodlot to provide unlimited firewood for free home heating. Although more expensive, videotapes and slide shows, covering a variety of topics from parenting to basic botany, are also available.

OTHER STATE STUFF

There are many state agencies that have free information but are not geared to deal with the public, as the Cooperative Extension is. In most cases these agencies may be found only in the central offices of the state capital. Many states have a Waste Management Board that can give you up-to-date information on recycling and reusing all sorts of consumer materials. For example, some state waste-management agencies will provide the Household Hazardous Waste Wheel free of charge. This is a circular slide rule that details all the options for reusing or recycling everything from paper to glass, metals, and toxic products. The agencies encourage home composting to reduce landfill burdens and are a good way to find out if there are local community composting programs or programs associated with nearby landfills. Brochures, booklets, and plentiful tips on conservation in the home are all distributed by these agencies.

Some states have a Water Resources Board, charged with the task of managing and delivering the public water supply. They often have extensive archives dealing with water-related issues such as flooding, aqueducts, groundwater, and a host of environmental and engineering subjects. These archives can be too technical for the public, but they may be the only source of information on specific subjects like domestic wells.

CITY GOVERNMENT

Few citizens realize that city and county governments prepare detailed guidelines for development, and many of these include mandatory landscaping ordinances. This is because after a park or avenue of street trees is planted, it becomes the responsibility of the Public Works Department. They are concerned with how trees influence street sweeping and the potential for root systems to damage pavement or invade city water and sewer pipes. Many cities and counties have developed a detailed city-street tree list of species considered well mannered and suitable for the community. The trees have also been reviewed for specific pests and diseases to ensure that the city tree community won't get sick in the future. Such a list is the best place to find out what trees are reliable and proven over the long term, and you can rest assured each cultivar has been thoroughly scrutinized. Call or visit city hall to obtain the tree lists free of charge from one or all of these departments: Public Works, Planning, Building, or Parks and Recreation. You may also find literature on water conservation, passive solar planting design, and a variety of other valuable subjects.

UTILITY COMPANIES

Your electric power and natural-gas supplies may come from local government or private companies. Many of these groups have ongoing programs that attempt to educate the public about ways they can reduce energy consumption. You may be surprised at how much free information they offer. For example, PG&E (Pacific Gas and Electric Co.) distributed free of charge the "Trees and Energy Conservation Calendar," a monthly wall calendar packed with well-written and useful information on various tree species, tree selection, and planting techniques; details on how landscaping influences microclimates around a home; and helpful diagrams of solar exposure in various seasons. Place a call to your local power company and inquire about materials available that are tailored to the needs of your local climate.

PRIVATE GROUPS

There has been a dramatic increase in the number of nonprofit private organizations across the nation that are involved with many issues important to our daily lives. Those dealing with subjects such as plants, soil, or the environment are excellent sources of free information. These groups are effective because they are not government-related and usually operate efficiently without the constraints of massive bureaucracies. In addition, there are associations that represent a particular profession and seek to further public understanding of their position and future directions. To do this, they prepare information materials, which can be obtained free or for a nominal fee.

Just a few of these resources are listed below, but you can get in touch with many more by keeping an eye out for advertisements and news releases. For example, the local newspaper may run a special story on Arbor Day, telling of the Arbor Day Foundation's efforts to encourage tree planting. Stories or announcements by the Audubon Society or Ducks Unlimited might lead you to free brochures on birds and their food plants. During periods of drought, newspapers may run stories on native plants that often reference local native-plant societies or similar environmental conservation groups. Look for these and many more in the advertising sections of gardening magazines or in general-interest glossies such as *Smithsonian* and *National Geographic*, which are on file at the public library. Using the library saves you money. Bring lots of change for the copier in case you find a good deal of juicy information.

AMERICAN FORESTS

The nation's oldest conservation group is actively involved in Global Releaf, an effort to plant trees that will ultimately affect climate and environmental quality. The group produces a tremendous amount of literature about how trees benefit individual homes as well as urban communities. To find out about their publications, write for information to: Global Releaf, P.O. Box 2000, Washington, DC 20013.

THE INTERNATIONAL SOCIETY OF ARBORICULTURE

Representing the tree care and preservation professionals, this is a nonprofit organization aimed at educating the public about trees and when a certified arborist should be consulted. The society now offers a series of free consumer brochures, which are well written and highly informative. Titles include *Benefits of Trees*, *Mature Tree Care*, *Tree Selection*, *Plant Health Care*, *New Tree Planting*, *Avoiding Tree & Utility Conflicts*, *Trees & Turf*, *Insect & Disease Problems*, *Recognizing Tree Hazards*, and *Why Hire an Arborist*. To request the brochures, write: International Society of Arboriculture, P.O. Box GG, Savoy, IL 61874-9411.

THE LAWN INSTITUTE

The Lawn Institute is also attempting to educate the public on how to take care of lawns. A well-educated consumer makes informed choices in turf-grass varieties, cares for turf with minimal chemical usage, and realizes the long-term value of grass to both visual and environmental quality. The institute's eight publications are free, but you must send $1 for postage with your request to: The Lawn Institute, 1509 Johnson Ferry Road, NE, Suite 190, Marietta, GA 30062-8122. Here are just a few examples of brochure titles:

- *How to Select the Best Grass Seed for Northern Lawns*
- *Home Lawn Care Programs That Work*
- *How the Environment Benefits from a Well-Maintained Lawn*
- *What You Need to Know About Proper Watering Practices*

GARDEN PROFESSIONALS

There are two types of professionals that can be of value in a budget garden. First are the advisers: garden designers, horticulturists, arborists, and other experts in their fields. Most charge fees for their services, usually by the hour. An exception, however, is with some nursery staff. A retail garden center wants to encourage you to buy their plants and employs salespeople who may come out to your house and make suggestions. This is ideal if you're not very experienced and know few plant names. Finding the right plant for the right place takes knowledge to ensure that it not only fits into the garden scheme but will grow successfully in that exposure, climate, and soil type. This may be a free service, or you may be required to make a minimum purchase first. But you'll have to ask, because some places don't advertise this or they'd be deluged with requests.

Another opportunity some seed sellers and nurseries offer is the free loan of seed spreaders and other equipment to help you plant a lawn or install sprinklers. These services are some of the best fringe benefits to paying slightly more for plants at a garden center. Other retail outlets may be less expensive but don't offer the extra services.

Junior colleges and universities with ornamental horticulture or landscape-architecture programs are packed with students who would love to make a little extra money on the side. Keep in mind that a first-year JC student is far less capable than a fourth-year ornamental-horticulture major. A good way to find student labor or help with design and plant selection is to contact the school placement office, which matches students with prospective employers, and can be a big help if you specify what your needs are. Plus, you don't have to make your name and phone number public, minimizing the risk of having strangers contact you directly.

BETTER-THAN-AVERAGE LITERATURE

Garden catalogs are discussed elsewhere in this book, but one of the most outstanding in terms of cheap or free information on perennials is Spring Hill Nurseries, 110 West Elm Street, Tipp City, Ohio 45371; phone (800) 582-8527. Spring Hill's color catalogs not only show clear photos of the individual plants, they also dedicate more than half their space to full-color renderings of actual perennial gardens matched to a corresponding plan-view diagram. They have been designed by gardening authority Derek Fell, and you can be certain they will be attractive and successful. One of the pitfalls in garden design is combining plants that have very different water and exposure needs, but Spring Hill plans have worked this out for you in detail. With such an enormous number of plants to choose from, most people don't have the training to put together sophisticated perennial color gardens such as these.

But there's more: Spring Hill guides you meticulously through the entire process of creating each garden. For example, the Versatile Corner Garden is clearly rendered utilizing just four plants: daylily, dwarf lilac, dwarf pink hydrangea, and blue fescue (an ornamental grass) to give it pizzazz. To obtain this kind of detail you would have to hire a professional, but Spring Hill lays it all out for you, including combinations of colors approved by the experts. Other plans in the catalog might include a butterfly and hummingbird garden, shade gardens, and rock-garden schemes.

CHEAP-SCAPES CHOICES: Magazines have a limited shelf life, which varies according to how frequently issues are published. Once an issue is outdated it can be discarded, particularly if it is a one-shot supplement. If you make friends with clerks in local grocery stores, bookstores, or other retail magazine sources in your area, they may be willing to donate old issues to your garden library rather than pitch them into the Dumpster. Remember, gardening information is never really out of date.

MAGAZINES

It helps to understand how magazines are sold to get the best value for your money. Publishers turn out magazines at different frequencies from once a week to seasonally or even once a year as a supplement. Many interiors or style magazines publish a single annual gardening supplement, which you'll find on newsstands in spring. These are usually packed with good gardening articles, although the quality of the photography varies and the material can sometimes be too general. But these publications also contain an assortment of advertisements that you can use to send for free catalogs and product information.

Landscape design has far more long-term appeal than interior-decorating trends.

Gardens mature over many years and are continually changing, yet they all share the timeless principles of horticulture. A story about maple trees written in 1940 is just as valuable as one published today, but if it's buried in an issue at the bottom of your stack, chances are you won't use it. A good way to clear out your storage space and salvage the usable information in back issues is to dissect them. Clip out articles you want to save and file them according to subject in a binder or filing cabinet. Use entire articles, clippings, and inspirational photos for future reference.

··

BEER-BUDGET ITEM: Gardening is a timeless activity that has changed little in the past fifty years. There have been literally thousands of books published on this subject, and today the market is flooded with new and very expensive titles. But if you haunt used bookstores, thrift stores, or garage sales, chances are you'll encounter older gardening books that are excellent references. Two useful titles that I find to be plentiful in used bookstores are *The New Garden Encyclopedia*, by E.L.D. Seymour, 1936; and *The Complete Book of Garden Magic*, by Roy E. Biles, 1935. Both of these books are great for reference and are well illustrated with line drawings; they usually sell for about $5 each. Note that this is about the price of a glitzy here-today-gone-tomorrow garden magazine.

··

A new issue of slick *Garden Design* magazine is a staggering $5, and though it contains beautiful photography, you should evaluate this investment by considering how much hard-core information is included. Certainly photographs are inspiring; they encourage us to get out and garden and can provide a graphic means of communicating design and style. Before you buy a magazine at this price it's important to study it to make sure it is suited to your gardening level. There are entire books you could buy for the cost of two issues. Or consider how many seed packets or seedling perennials you could buy for the price of one magazine. Budget gardeners know that these little expenditures add up, and it's sometimes too easy to fall into the trap of being penny-wise and pound-foolish.

APPENDIX

TAXES: WHEN IT'S TIME TO SELL YOUR HOUSE

 If you sell your home, then buy another of *equal or greater value* within a designated time period, the Internal Revenue Service does not levy a capital-gains tax on your profit. But when the kids grow up and move away, many people sell their large family homes and buy something smaller, realizing a considerable profit in the process. That profit will be taxed if the new home costs less, unless you are over fifty-five and choose to use the one-time capital-gains-tax exemption allowed by the IRS. But if you do not take this exemption, you'll need all the deductions you can muster to reduce the tax liability. For example, if you sold the family home for $175,000 and purchased a new home for $125,000, you would have to pay taxes on the profit margin of $50,000.

What so many people fail to realize is that the cost of certain documented home improvements can be deducted from the taxable profit, thus reducing your tax liability. If in the above example you replaced the roof for $8,000, added central air conditioning for $3,000, and built a deck for $5,000, the total of these investments would be subtracted from your profit margin, reducing it to only $34,000. For this reason it is essential you keep very detailed records of certain improvements so they can be used later on when you sell. You may end up with ten to twenty years of improvements, but you'll be glad to have them when the tax man cometh. Whenever possible, save receipts and check numbers for any of the following deductible improvements.

DEDUCTIBLE HOME IMPROVEMENTS

Escrow costs of purchasing or refinancing, title insurance premiums, transfer taxes, and recording fees

Significant roof replacement

Architect's fees for a *completed* project

Construction costs of an addition

Construction costs of an in-ground swimming pool

Underground sprinkler systems

Electrical installation

Plumbing installation

New flooring, including linoleum, tile, or carpeting

New installed appliances such as dishwasher, stove, water heater, or furnace

Decking and patios

Installed lighting that is permanent

Solar heating units

Wood or garden sheds

Vinyl siding

Fencing

Sizable concrete, brickwork, or paving

Central heat or air-conditioning installation

Large-scale landscaping (document with photos)

NOT DEDUCTIBLE

Aboveground pool

Minor plumbing or electrical repairs

Painting

Plastering

Wallpapering

Replacement of rain gutters

Small-scale plantings

Portable air-conditioning units

Garage-door openers

Replacement of broken windows and screens

Spot roof repairs

Also keep in mind that every mature tree in your landscape is valuable, a factor recognized by the IRS. If you lose a big tree to disease or a storm, you may be entitled to a tax break or compensation for the loss by your home-insurance company. Call the adjustor and a certified arborist, and photograph the tree *before* it is removed to document the loss. The arborist will be able to determine the value of the tree in writing, which is helpful later on when negotiating with the IRS or insurance adjustor. Remember: Just as you use photographs to document your household valuables, take photos of your landscape every few years to show its maturity and value.

BIBLIOGRAPHY

Bryant, Jeoff. *Propagation Handbook: Basic Techniques for Gardeners*. Mechanicsburg, PA: Stackpole Books, 1995.

Bubel, Nancy, *The New Seed Starters Handbook*. Emmaus, PA: Rodale Press, 1988.

Hansen, Michael, Ph.D., and the editors of Consumer Reports Books. *Pest Control for Home and Garden*. Yonkers, NY: Consumer Reports Books, 1993.

Klien, Hilary Dole, and Adrian M. Wenner. *Tiny Game Hunting: Environmentally Healthy Ways to Trap and Kill the Pests in Your House and Garden*. New York: Bantam Books, 1991.

Park, George. *Park's Success with Seeds*. Park Seed Company. P.O. Box 31, Highway 254, Greenwood, SC 29648-0031.

Thompson, Peter. *The Propagator's Handbook*. British, 1993.

Yepsen, Roger B., Jr. ed. *Organic Plant Protection*. Emmaus, PA: Rodale Press, 1976.

INDEX